99 Minute Millionaire

The Simplest and Easiest Book Ever on Getting Started Investing and Becoming Rock Star Rich

Scott Alan Turner

ISBN 0692758097
ISBN-13 978-0692758090

To my wife, Katie, the real rock star.

*To the **Financial Rock Star** nation. It's your show, and this is your book. Many thanks to you all. You rock!*

Contents

Introduction...1

PART 1 Having More Money: Would You Rather Live on Steak and Lobster, or Peanut Butter and Jelly? 15

1. Storing Up Grain in Silos.....................................17
2. Ninety-seven Slices of Bread..........................22
3. More Food Than You Could Ever Eat 25
4. Are You Smarter Than a Bagel? I Wasn't.....................30
5. Waiting for the Dough to Rise.....................33
6. A $64,000 Pizza and a $1,421,141 Car 37
7. Cleaning Out the Fridge.............................40
8. Eating Out for Every Meal.............................45

PART 2 Foundations of Investing: Basic Cooking Skills 49
9. The Chocolate Caramel Crunchy Clusters Business 51
10. The Failure of Chocolate-Covered Green Beans 56
11. Big Carts, Little Carts, Flat Carts, Kid Carts 61

12. What Goes in the Carts? 64

13. Where Do Groceries Come From? 69

14. Donuts—Is There Anything They Can't Do? 73

15. The Food Buffets of the World 77

16. Buying a Piece of Every Fruit 82

PART 3 Becoming a Successful Investor: Selecting the Freshest, Highest-quality Ingredients at the Lowest Cost 87

17. Would You Eat Cow Stomach? 89

18. Oh No—Mad Cow and E. Coli! 93

19. Living in Happyland, in a Gumdrop House on Lollipop Lane 96

20. New and Improved Flavors vs. Plain Ol' Vanilla 98

21. The 5-Star Restaurant That's Serving Dog Food 100

22. Low-Cost, Well-Diversified Meals 105

23. How Much Is It to Run a Kitchen? 108

24. Creating a Balanced Meal Plan for a Long, Healthy Life 113

25. I'm Young, Why Can't I Just Eat Cake All the Time? 123

26. Picnics in Winter 126

27. When Choconuts Goes Bankrupt 133

28. My Eyes Were Bigger Than My Stomach 135

29. Biting Off More Than You Can Chew 138

30. Getting Gobbled 140

PART 4 Managing Your Money Like a Pro: Fad Diets That Leave Your Wallet Weighing Less....................................143

31. Try This Hot, New Restaurant—It's Amazing!...........145

32. Rachel Ray's Picture on the Box Doesn't Mean It's the Best Chicken Stock 148

33. Loaded Baked Potatoes 151

34. Voted Best-Tasting Burger Since 1934! 154

35. Premium Grocery Store Shelf Space 157

PART 5 How to Beat Wall Street: A Recipe for Success. 159

36. Store-Bought or Homemade? 161

37. How Long to Age Cheese and Wine 162

38. Frozen Pizza..165

39. Pizza Delivery 170

40. Rolling Your Own Dough 173

41. Pizza, Pizza, or Pizza? 179

42. Gordon Ramsay, Chef-Boyardee, or You? 182

43. Attending Cooking Classes.. 190

44. Shopping at ALDI...192

45. Lunch at the Office Cafeteria........................196

46. Are You Getting Enough Veggies? 199

47. Good Cooking Takes Time.........................202

48. Is This a Secret Recipe?............................206

49. The Great Chefs of the World.........................209

50. Advanced Cooking Techniques 213

51. Cooking at Home Once in a While..........................216

52. The Icing on the Cake.................................218

Free Dessert.........................221

Appendix A: Master of Cookies........................223

Appendix B: The Word on Index Funds 227

References.........................235

Websites and Services Mentioned 239

Acknowledgments 241

About the Author..........................243

Introduction

Back in my money-moron days, around the year 2000, I followed a lot of bad investing advice.

I lost $40,000 in the stock market by foolishly thinking I knew what I was doing.

I went from money moron at age 22 to self-made millionaire, thirteen years later at age 35. Part of achieving that goal was following the investing principles I share in this book. I socked away a lot of money during those thirteen years to have that much to invest. And over the next several decades that money will continue to grow even more. I'm throwing out there my financial situation not to impress anyone, but simply to impress upon you that if I can do it, you can too.

What is "investing"?

It's putting your money to work so that it makes you more money (and rich)—that's investing. If you don't know what "putting your money to work" means or how to do that—don't worry. That's what I'll help you with in this book!

I don't want you to make the same mistakes I did. Since losing that first chunk of money in the stock market, I've educated myself by reading over 200 personal finance and investing books, university research papers, and the works of Nobel prize winners on the subject of investing. My wife Katie and I have also worked with a fee-only Certified Financial Planner since 2005, starting shortly after we were married.

After **losing** a lot, I've **learned** a lot.

I now spend 60 to 90 minutes a *year* reviewing my investments. I'd rather spend my free time helping people with their financial questions, playing with my twin toddlers, cooking amazing hamburgers for my wife and our friends, and playing guitar in my band.

Investing has been made out to be such a complex topic that you might believe it requires a PhD in economics to get started or to build wealth, but once you get past the jargon, it's simple. You might be so afraid of losing money (so am I!), you end up making terrible money decisions that will cost you tens to hundreds of thousands of dollars over your lifetime. Do any of the following sound familiar?

- What is investing?

- I don't know how to get started investing.

- I'm young, why should I invest?

- I'm older, is it too late for me to invest?

- Investing is too complex.

- I don't have a lot of money to invest.

- I don't have *any* money to invest, I'm just trying to pay my bills.

- Investing is boring.

- Investing is for rich people.

- I don't have time to learn how to invest.

- I want someone else to manage my money for me.

- There are too many choices to pick from.

- I'm afraid of losing my money.

Or as one listener wrote in to my show, *Financial Rock Star*—"I've been reading up as much as I can [on investing], but some of these topics seem to send me in an endless circle of searching with no real answers, sadly."

If you are new to investing—welcome! You're in a great spot because you haven't had the chance to lose all the money I have by being stupid (more on that later). If you are not new to investing, you'll still get something out of this book, even if it's just the ability to learn how to explain to others investing in simple language.

One of the biggest problems investors face is financial experts who make this stuff seem more complex than it is. You occasionally find someone that simplifies it, but they may give out bad, inaccurate, or incomplete advice. We are bombarded with advertisements and news every day about what we should be doing with our money. There are stories, articles, products, and salespeople pitching how we can strike it rich if we just follow certain advice.

You will either find yourself very confused or very scared. Confused over what to do and scared to lose your money. You may have even lost money already and are afraid of getting back in the game. I'll strip away all those layers of complexity and replace your fear with confidence.

This is a book that answers your questions about investing in a simple, easy-to-understand way. This book has been designed to guide you, step-by-step, through the technical jargon and make you a more successful investor than 95% of Wall Street professionals *who have finance degrees.*

This book is for people who want to achieve financial freedom, whatever that means to you.

- Is it being able to retire early?

- Is it paying for your kid's college tuition?

- Is it buying your parents a home?

- Is it quitting your job and pursuing something else you're passionate about?

- Is it taking a year off and traveling the world?

- Is it being crazy generous and helping people?

What would you do if money didn't matter? Financial freedom means different things to different people. I'll show you how to get there from an investing perspective. What you choose to do with that additional money is up to you.

I know what you might be thinking: "Why should I believe anyone that doesn't have any fancy title or formal education in investing?"

Great question!

I have no training or work experience dealing with the financial markets or the industry in which they operate. I've never worked on Wall Street or for a Wall Street firm. I am not a stockbroker. I'm not a financial planner. I don't have a finance degree. There are no acronyms after my name.

But one of the things you will discover in this book is the people that have those things often give out flawed advice that costs you money, and they aren't really that good at investing.

What I do have is the ability to teach and to learn. And everything I have learned, I will share with you, citing university studies, academic research, and Nobel prize-winning economists. In other words—I'm not making this stuff up and pulling it out of thin air. It's not *Scott's investing philosophy*. It's *Scott sharing documented academic research made by people much smarter than he is, so you can understand it simply and easily.*

Someone can have CPA, CFP, MBA, RIA, or Vice President after their name, and still give lousy advice. Just because someone has an impressive title doesn't mean they have your best interest in mind. I did get an A in financial accounting during the one semester I was in graduate school. That must count for something, right? No, it doesn't. If you feel more comfortable hearing from someone with an impressive title, fine—I'm the CEO of Enterprise Innovation Group. Number of employees: one. Me.

You have a choice to make, and if you get it wrong you're in trouble.

- You can trust the people trying to make money off you (banks, brokers, many advisors, insurance agents, investment companies)

- You can trust your friends, neighbors, and co-workers who may be as in the dark as you are about money but want you to think they are smart

- You can trust academic research, which doesn't want your money or care what you think about it

If there is **one thing** that separates me from other people offering investment advice, it is this:

Unlike people who make money if you buy a product or service, make a commission, a kickback, an endorsement, a referral fee, or whatever, I have nothing to sell you (other than some proven investing advice guaranteed to save you thousands of dollars). I get compensated in the form of thank-you emails by helping you do well (and whatever you paid for this book unless you're reading it at the library right now for free).

You won't find in this book the next hot stock tip mentioned by the entertainers in nightly business shows. You won't hear the same advice that celebrity financial gurus give out about how to invest your money. Not only is their advice incomplete and inaccurate, often they offer conflicting advice and don't invest themselves in the products they push onto you.

The advice in this book is a proven path to growing your money, backed by academics, research, and university studies, not marketing hype.

And frankly, I'm going to keep things simple using fifth-grade math, pulling a few numbers from reports, and explaining a handful of definitions. No Wall Street background needed. It's not rocket science. If it were, you wouldn't understand it anyway, and I wouldn't bother trying to explain it.

Decades-Old Advice

The same investing philosophy in this book is practiced by tens of thousands of do-it-yourself investors every day to build wealth and retire early. Many financial advisors, as well as large institutional investors (those that manage billions of dollars of investments), also follow this same advice for their clients as part of their investment strategy and retirement planning. It's not just some investing plan I made up.

In fact, the advice has been around since 1974. But the reason you don't hear about it is because it's kind of a **boring** way to invest. It doesn't take a lot of time to learn, maintain, or keep up-to-date on. Can you spare an hour a year to become a successful investor?

I don't use the phrase "get rich" very often because it sounds scammy, like I'm trying to sell you a secret, undiscovered goldmine. The process in this book is used to get rich slowly, not quickly. It works!

Fifth-grade Simple

I've intentionally made this book **fifth-grade simple**. Why? Because after looking at all of the "best'" and "top-selling" investing books for beginners around, after reading just one or two pages in the introductions, I would come across the same stuff about "rates of return" and the "stock market goes up overtime." See! I just did it too. I too was left scratching my head and asking myself, "I'm only on page two, and I'm seeing special terms a regular person may not understand. Why continue on to page three?"

So this is the challenge I laid down for myself:

Teach a person who has zero finance knowledge about investing, and make them a better investor than the people working on Wall Street. Oh yeah, and do it in 99 minutes in such simple language they could explain it to a fifth grader.

There are just a handful of principles that, once you learn them, will get you 95+ percent of the way there. And at the end, if you want to take it up a notch and move on to more advanced topics, the choice is yours.

If you will stay with me and follow the steps in this book, you and your family will build wealth through investing. I think you'll be very surprised just how easy it is to be a successful investor and have all of the financial freedom that comes from it.

It doesn't matter if you have $10, $100, or $100,000 to invest. You will be a better investor than the vast majority of the people around you, and you'll be able to explain the most important investing topics in a simple, easy-to-understand manner.

A Bright Future

Don't be the person who gets to retirement age only to find that you need to keep working—*until you die*. Or the person who has to live on peanut butter and jelly sandwiches in their golden years. I *love* PB&J, it's one of my favorite meals, but I choose to eat it because I *want* to, not because I *have* to. Be the kind of person who **never** stresses out about money and lives comfortably and worry-free.

The Fast Lane to Expertise

What you're about to learn about investing has been proven to build wealth, without you having to spend hours of your time learning. All you have to do to gain control of your future is to keep reading. Each chapter will give you new insights and arm you with the skills to have financial freedom. I challenge you to take control of your life right now, create the future you deserve, and reap the rewards in your life for the decades to come.

One final note: I want to thank you for reading this far, and I congratulate you. Only 28% of people read a nonfiction book each year.[1] *And 10% of people who buy a book never finish it.*

Your money is important. And even though I don't know you, and we've never met, it's important to me that you keep as much of your money as you can and make as much investing as you can. I've made a lot of money mistakes, and I would hate for you to repeat what I did and lose money. I hate to lose money, and I hate to see other people lose money when they don't have to or when others get ripped off. It's my mission to educate you and anyone that will listen and learn the difference between fact and fairytale advice.

If you and I were sitting down for coffee together, it's the same advice I would tell you in person. It's the same advice I give on my show, *Financial Rock Star*. It's the same advice I've followed for the past fifteen years (with a few hiccups along the way . . .).

If you do not finish this book, front to back, I guarantee you will be costing yourself thousands, to even hundreds of thousands, of dollars over your lifetime.

That's your money! Commit to spending the time to read the whole book. Every chapter has action items you can do to get closer to your goals. Share with others what you are discovering and applying because one of the best ways for you to learn and remember something is by teaching it to someone else. So, teaching it to others will raise the odds you will reach your financial goals.

Turn the page and let me show you how to become a smart investor.

What This Book Is NOT

Your time is valuable, and I don't want to waste it. I made a lot of promises in the Introduction as to what this book is. But I also want to be clear on what this book is not, so you can decide if it's right for you.

—*This book is NOT complicated.*

Complicated doesn't help you. And if it's not simple, you won't do it or understand it. When you win, I win because I want to see you succeed.

—*This book is NOT going to mislead you with half-baked information.*

I believe in whole-baked information. You may have heard you can get a 12% return on your money (it's early, but I'll explain "returns" in part 1. It's how your money can make you more money). I use real math, backed by academic research, and I provide the resources, so you can check the facts on your own. While some people trying to get your money want to convince you a 12% return is reality, I'll peel back the layers showing why 12%

returns are as likely as finding a fat-free donut that results in weight loss.

—This book is NOT something that hasn't been said before.

As you will see repeatedly throughout the book, the information is based on decades of academic research using data going back to 1926. What I've done is taken information that is made out to be complex and confusing, and presented it in simple, plain English.

—This book is NOT a get-rich-quick scheme.

Let me be clear—this book is NOT a get-rich-quick scheme. I will show you how to get rich slowly. If you want quick, go to Vegas.

—This book is NOT a sales pitch.

You can't write an investment book without talking about investments. So I included some of my favorite low-cost products and services that I recommend you check out.

Neither I, my book publisher, nor anyone involved in this book has a financial stake in any product, investment, or service mentioned. No compensation has been received, no kickbacks, no advertising money, no commissions, and no referral fees.

Where there are comparable low-cost alternatives, they were included.

—This book is NOT just for people with money.

It's for anyone who wants to build wealth. If you have $1, $100, $100,000, or $1,000,000—the song remains the same. These simple principles are critical to start applying in your finances. Even if you think you know them all already—it's time to make sure you take action and follow the principles. We all start where we start, and go from there. The opportunity is for everyone.

—This book is NOT wrong.

The content in this book is grounded in research from academia— university professors with PhDs, Nobel prize-winning economists, etc. I'm not giving you my opinion, just the best information from the smartest people in the world.

While you can contact me and tell me I'm wrong, my reply is going to be the same—you're going to have to go argue with that Nobel laureate, it's their research. Good luck.

In the next section, you'll have to decide if you want a steak-and-lobster style retirement or if you'll be stuck eating peanut butter and jelly for thirty years, or being a Walmart greeter.

—This book IS for you to

- *get out of debt faster,*

- *save more money, and*

- *retire rich.*

PART 1

Having More Money:

Would You Rather Live on Steak and Lobster,

or Peanut Butter and Jelly?

1. Storing Up Grain in Silos

My dad spent 33 years working for the town on the roads and eight years painting tools in a factory. My mom has lived in the same two thousand-person small town all her life, having the same lifelong friends she went to elementary school with. They lived a very simple life, never owned a home, never had any debts, and rarely traveled. When my dad passed away, Mom moved into a government-subsidized retirement community. Her only income is from social security.

She doesn't like traveling, doesn't want a home, could care less about fancy clothes, and doesn't eat out much. She takes the sen citizen bus to Walmart because she doesn't like driving anymore either. Don't get me wrong—she's as happy as a clam. She has no wants other than to see her family and friends.

But this is not my picture of retirement for myself. I plan on traveling—a lot (Europe is my favorite destination, I've been four times). I'm an early retiree. I work because I want to, not because I have to. If I were age 65, retirement would not be possible on social security. Heck, I couldn't even pay the property taxes on my house with social security.

And this is why I started saving money at an early age. I saved *early*. I saved *often*. And I saved *a lot*. In the one year my wife and I lived with our in-laws, we saved **90% of our income.**

Why should you save money? A big reason we can all agree on is— to buy things! What those things are differ from person to person, and it isn't always *stuff*.

When you have savings, a world of opportunity opens up. Just think about it:

- Working at a job you love

- Not working at all

- Taking a year off

- Living wherever you want

- Saving for college

- Buying a new car with cash

- Having an emergency fund in case of a job loss or medical emergency

- Spending more time with friends and family

- Buying stuff

- Helping people (one of the great joys of having extra money is being able to help those that don't)

- Having choices and freedom in retirement

- Having choices and freedom *now*

Put simply, investing is putting away money for future use, usually at least for five years into the future, in expectation that the amount you put away will grow more than what you put in. You might have been asked before, "Are you saving for a rainy day? Are you saving for your future? Are you saving for retirement?"

You need money both now (for expenses), in a few years (saving), and in the future (investing).

Good savings habits can begin in children as early as three years old. Developing your savings habits now—no matter what your age—will result in huge paybacks later.

Your retirement is coming. It may be 20, 30, or 40 years away. *You can't stop it from coming.* Plan for retirement, and you'll be able to ease into it under your control. Do little to nothing to get ready, and retirement may run you over like a freight train. Those who are financially ill-prepared for retirement, in just a few years, may see their money gobbled up by rising property taxes, increased health care costs, and inflation. Suddenly, they have to sell their home to get some money and then move in with the kids just to survive, which is fine if that's the goal, but if it isn't, start planning now, so you can own what your retirement will look like.

How do you picture your retirement and do you have a plan to get there? The fast answer is it's going to take money. And unless you want to live in a government-subsidized retirement community like my mom, you're going to need a lot of it.

And I won't sugarcoat it—saving takes time. An event happens, and you'll get off course. You'll have to find your way back. Birds don't travel in straight lines. They go over, under, and around objects. They make adjustments and get back on course. Later chapters will show you the pot holes, detours, speed traps, and how to avoid them to keep you going in the straightest line possible, like geese heading south for the winter.

Saving Rates

The **current** savings rate for a person living in the US is 5.4%[2]. Compare that to Europe, where the savings rate is 12.7%.

It's shocking that despite the United States' being the richest country in the world, it has some of the brokest citizens. The answer to why is because of how much we spend on *stuff*.

Estimates put you needing 70% to 80% of your yearly income to live on in retirement. **Some experts say you'll need 100% of your yearly income in retirement to live on.** So if you're making the average $53,000 in household income a year and spending it all, you will need $37,000 per year in retirement to keep your current standard of living. Figure you want to retire at age 65, and you'll live to age 85, that's $742,000 you'll need.

Research shows the average 40-year-old American has only $63,000 saved for retirement. This falls well short of conservative benchmarks of a nest egg being three times a person's annual salary. If you're making $55,000, you should have a balance of $165,000 already in the bank.

The average 50-year-old has just $117,000 saved for retirement. In your fifties, the goal is to have a minimum of four to six times your annual salary saved. If you make $60,000 a year, you should have at least $240,000 socked away.

What that means is most people are not saving enough.

While social security can *sometimes* be enough to get by on (as my mom does), you're going to have a pretty scaled-down life if that's your retirement plan. No house. No travel. No new cars. No eating out all the time. And if you plan on living someplace expensive, like New York City, forget about it.

Your Next Step: Ask a close friend or family member, "What would you do if money were no object?"

Now that you know saving is incredibly important, you might think putting your money in a savings account would be a great idea. Wrong! Let's take a quick look at why saving up cash and doing nothing with it *will* cause you to *lose* money.

2. Ninety-seven Slices of Bread

If you bought a 100-slice loaf of bread for $10, next year you would only be able to buy 97 slices with the same $10.

How is that possible? The cost of things goes up over time.

When I was a kid, I loved riding my bike to the store to buy candy (okay, I did this almost every day in the summer). I remember a pack of gum was $0.25. Currently in the checkout line at Walmart, a pack of gum is $0.79, and maybe even $0.99, depending on if you're buying Orbitz vs. Big Red.

Prices have gone up. Prices on stuff always go up. Think of something you bought as a kid and how much that thing costs now. It's more expensive, right? Even if you are 18 years old, that thing you bought when you were eight costs more.

That price increase is called "inflation." Stuff goes up in price, over time. On average prices go up 3% each year. We won't get into why. It's just one of those facts of life. It's why if I had 75 cents, I could buy one pack of gum today, but as a kid, I would have been able to buy three packs of gum with the same amount of money.

In other words, given the exact same amount of money, you can buy less stuff as you get older.

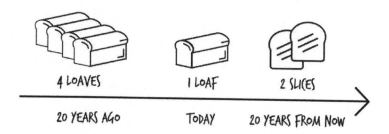

If you took $20,000, which would have bought you a house in the 1960s, and stuck it in a cookie jar for 50 years, today that $20,000 would only buy you the front porch. Or maybe just the driveway. But no house.

It's necessary for your money to at least keep pace with inflation, which means growing by 3% a year—so your money can keep up with the rising costs of living.

Making Money Sowing Seeds

Say you have a friend who wants to start a farm. Your friend asks you to give them $100, so they can buy some vegetable seeds, and in return they will give you back $10 every year, forever.

At the end of the first year, your friend's seeds have grown into plants. They sell the vegetables, make some money, and you get $10. So what percent do you get every year? Ten percent. Because $10 is 10% of $100. This 10% is called your "rate of return."

How fast your money grows each year is the "rate" at which it grows. The growth rate. Or what you will more commonly hear—the "rate of return" or "annual return." It's very important and one of the foundations of being a smart investor. But this number alone *isn't* the whole story, and it's where most investors end up losing.

"Rate of return" differs from another term called the "interest rate," which is the rate you pay to borrow money, like for a student loan.

Your Next Step: Find an older person and ask them how much they paid for a pack of gum when they were younger, a loaf of bread, or a gallon of milk. Compare that to what you pay today.

You now understand why putting money in a cookie jar will not help you achieve financial security. Next it's time to understand how to make your money grow to keep it from losing its buying power.

3. More Food Than You Could Ever Eat

If you were given the choice between getting $1 million right now or taking a penny now and doubling the amount every day for the next 30 days, what would you choose? If you're like 90% of people, you would take the $1 million. But you would be shortchanging yourself by $4 million. If you took a penny and doubled the amount for 30 days, the balance would be $5,368,709.12. That is the power of compounding, or "compound interest."

Take a look at this chart showing 30 days of magic penny doubling.

Day	Value ($)
1	0.01
2	0.02
3	0.04
4	0.08
5	0.16
6	0.32
7	0.64
8	1.28
9	2.56
10	5.12
11	10.24
12	20.48
13	40.96
14	81.92
15	163.84
16	327.68
17	655.36
18	1,310.72
19	2,621.44
20	5,242.88
21	10,485.76
22	20,971.52
23	41,943.04
24	83,886.08
25	167,772.16
26	335,544.32
27	671,088.64
28	1,342,177.28
29	2,684,354.56
30	5,368,709.12

Compounding—At Work

If you invest $100 and get a rate of return of 10%, that $100 creates $10 for you, so you now have $110.

What if the same thing happens again? Is the new amount $120? No.

You get a 10% return on $110, which is $121.

A lousy buck? Yes, but this is a small amount in a short example.

Let's see what happens if you compound different amounts over long periods of time—the type of savings you could do as you start saving and as the money you earn at your job increases over time.

Years to compound	$100/month	$500/month	$1000/month
5	$7,657	$38,282	$76,562
10	$19,988	$99,934	$199,866
15	$39,848	$199,226	$398,448
16	$45,087	$225,419	$450,833
17	$50,850	$254,231	$508,457
18	$57,189.	$285,924	$571,843
19	$64,162	$320,787	$641,568
20	$71,832	$359,136	$718,265
21	$80,269	$401,320	$802,633

22	$89,551	$447,722	$895,436
23	$99,760	$498,765	$997,521
24	$110,990	$554,911	$1,109,813
25	$123,343	$616,673	$1,233,335
26	$136,931	$684,610	$1,369,209
27	$151,878	$759,342	$1,518,671
28	$168,320	$841,546	$1,683,079
29	$186,407	$931,971	$1,863,927
30	$206,301	$1,031,439	$2,062,860

The real power of compounding doesn't show up in the beginning. When you have small amounts, the compounding is small. But after many years, when the amounts are huge, the growth is astounding. If you look at that table, you will see after 15 years of saving $500 a month and compounding, you've got barely $100,000. Only enough to live on for a few years. And after saving for 20 years, you might feel the same way—the amount has barely tripled. But the real growth is in the later years. From year 25 to 30, just five years, the amount grows from $684,610 to over $1 million. A jump of over $300,000 in just five years.

To build wealth, you have to have patience.

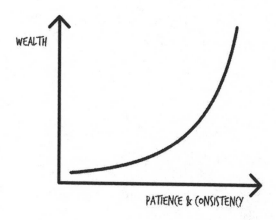

As an investor you want to take advantage of the power of compounding. How long you invest your money, so it can compound, makes a huge difference. I thought I knew all about it, and next I share how I thought I was smarter than Albert Einstein.

4. Are You Smarter Than a Bagel? I Wasn't

Have you heard of Albert Einstein?

He was a pretty smart guy.

What do you think one of the smartest people that ever lived had to say about compound interest?

> *Compound interest is the greatest mathematical discovery of all time.*

> *Compound interest is the eighth wonder of the world. He who understands it, earns it . . . he who doesn't . . . pays it.*

Those are some powerful words from an undisputed genius.

> *I am so smart. I am so smart. S-m-r-t. I mean s-m-a-r-t.*

> —Homer Simpson

I thought I was a pretty smart when I was twenty years old. In fact, I thought I was smarter than my college professor Dr. Muchado. One day when we were talking, he was giving me some advice for when I graduated:

"Save 10% of what you earn when you graduate."

I will never forget my response:

"Ha! Why would I save 10% when I'm 20? I'll just save 20% when I'm 40."

If you're young and brilliant like I was and know that you're smarter than your parents and everyone older than you, please hear me on this:

<u>Dumb Me</u>

Dumb Me told Dr. Muchado I would save 20% of my income starting at age 40, instead of 10% at age 20. I blew off his suggestion of saving 10% when I graduated from college.

Dumb Me:

- Starts saving $5,000 a year at age 40.

- Adds another $5,000 a year until age 65. (25 years of contributions)

- Invests a total of $125,000.

Through the power of compound interest with a rate of return at 10%, the amount Dumb Me would have at age 65 is $572,066.

In this scenario, I would have invested twice as much money each year and for an additional 15 years compared to if I had started investing at age 20 (read on to see what I mean!).

Smart Me

Smart Me would have listened to older and wiser people, despite my knowing far more than they did (of course!).

Smart Me:

- Starts saving $2,500 a year at age 20.

- Adds another $2,500 a year until age 30. (10 years of contributions)

- Invests a total of $25,000

Through the power of compound interest with a rate of return at 10% the amount Smart Me would have at age 65 is $1,612,622.

I guess Smart Me wasn't so smart. Good call, Dr. Muchado.

If compound interest is such a great thing and Einstein called it the eighth wonder of the world, why do so few people take full advantage of it? You'll need to know how to make it work for you. Read on . . .

5. Waiting for the Dough to Rise

If you've ever made your own pizza or bread dough, part of the process is waiting for the dough to rise before you can bake it. Sometimes it takes a couple of hours, so it's a good idea to get dinner started early. What you are about to discover is that compounding works the same way—start early and be patient to reap the greatest rewards later on.

Compounding is a power that makes you lots of money.

There are three important factors that make compounding work for you:

1.   How much money you put aside to grow

2.   How long that money grows

3.   The rate at which the money grows

Here is an example of **$100 compounding at different rates:**

Year	5%	8%	10%
10	$1,320	$1,564	$1,753
20	$3,471	$4,942	$6,300
30	$6,976	$12,234	$18,094

| 40 | $12,683 | $27,978 | $48,685 |
| 50 | $21,981 | $61,967 | $128,029 |

Not very interesting, right? That's just a lousy $100.

But now let's see what happens if you put in $100 a month.

Year	5%	8%	10%
10	$15,499	$18,128	$20,146
20	$40,746	$57,266	$72,399
30	$81,870	$141,761	$207,929
40	$148,856	$324,180	$559,460
50	$257,970	$718,009	$1,471,242

Your Next Step: Use my Investment Calculator at ScottAlanTurner.com. Enter in the dollar amount you would like to invest each month and see how much it will be worth at different rates of compounding.

$1M by the Age of 65 . . .

Let's say you found a way to compound your money and earn a 10% return. How much would you have to save each month to have $1M by age 65?

Starting Age	Investment per month	Total amount put away (principal)	Total interest (through compounding)
15	$57	$34,638	$965,499
20	$95	$51,516	$948,514
25	$158	$75,902	$924,124
30	$263	$110,628	$889,406
35	$442	$159,256	$840,743
40	$753	$226,104	$773,903
45	$1,316	$316,053	$683,951
50	$2,412	$434,289	$565,711
55	$4,881	$585,808	$414,191
60	$12,913	$774,823	$225,177

Crazy, right? A 20-year-old only has to save $51,516 over 45 years while a 45-year-old has to save $316,053 over 20 years.

Consider the following chart showing the benefits of saving early. The example uses a compounding rate of 7%.

Kourtney (small dotted line) starts investing at age 35, and invests $5,000 each year until age 65. In total, she invests $150,000. Her money compounds to $540,741.

Khloe (medium dotted line) invests $5,000 each year between age 25 to 35, then stops. In total she invests $50,000. Her money compounds to $602,070.

Kim (solid line) invests $5,000 each year between age 25 to 65. In total she invests $200,000. Her money compounds to $1,142,811.

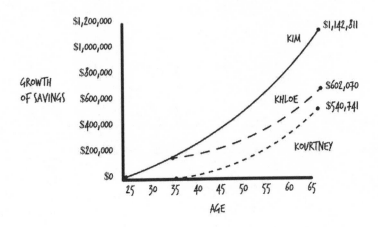

Your Next Step: If you are young, go find someone around retirement age (60 or more) and ask them if they wish they had started saving sooner. If you are around retirement age, go find someone young and explain to them the eighth wonder of the world using the example of doubling your pennies.

So, the amount of money, how long it compounds, and the rate at which it compounds are the three ingredients of compounding power.

At this point, you might be asking yourself, "Where am I going to get the money?" Let me tell you about my $1,421,141 car.

6. A $64,000 Pizza and a $1,421,141 Car

Have you ever eaten a $64,000 pizza?

Actually—you have.

A delicious cheese pizza costs about $13.21 on average.[3] If you buy one with pepperoni topping and eat out once a week from ages 18 to 43, you'll spend $17,220 on pizza. If you skip the pizza and invest the money instead, compounding at 9% for 25 years, you'll have $64,000.

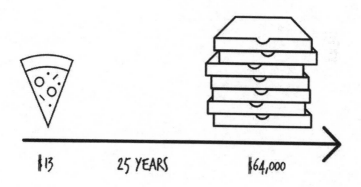

$13   25 YEARS $64,000

A lot of people believe they will never be able to retire or will retire deep in debt. This situation often comes from poor decisions made very early in life. I should know because I made the **same** exact ones (you might have too).

The poor decisions aren't intentional. You just don't have basic knowledge of saving, budgeting, and planning. In our teen years at home, few of us learn how to manage money. We spend money as fast as we make it. Moms and dads may say, "Save your money," although little else is taught to us. This was my case. The early years of adulthood, living on our own, is the time when we start to get real money lessons, and we often learn the hard way.

About a year after starting my first job out of college, I went out and bought a brand-new red Jeep Bigfoot Edition. Not too much longer after that I bought a used Porsche. I've done the math on the money I spent on these two vehicles.

Jeep insurance	$2,900
Porsche depreciation and loan interest	$15,000
Jeep depreciation	$9,000
Porsche insurance	$2,000
Totally awesome car stereo	$2,500
Total	**$31,400**
Value of money if it were invested for 20 years @ 10% interest	**$211,244**
Value of money if it were invested for 40 years @ 10% interest	**$1,421,141**

I owned both of those vehicles before I was 25 years old.

Did you know the average price of a new car is $31,000? And 99% of new cars are bought by borrowing money from a bank or lender to pay for the car (financed). The average amount financed is $29,000. Not that much different than the $31,400 I spent on my first two cars.

The quickest way to $1M is to buy used cars (preferably at least 3 years old) and drive them until the wheels fall off. If I had kept driving my old car and waited a few years until I bought my junky truck, I would have an extra million dollars in the bank at age 65.

You might think you don't have $200 to $300 to save each month, but if you are like I was, the money is probably sitting in your driveway in the form of a car payment (or in your mouth in the form of a slice of pizza!). Ouch! Also, the more expensive the car, you pay higher property taxes and costlier auto insurance. Compounding can work for you, but before it can, there are a few things to get straightened out first, which I cover next.

7. Cleaning Out the Fridge

In his book *The Millionaire Next Door*, Thomas J. Stanley interviews a thousand millionaires to discover their habits and how they built their wealth.

It's one of my favorite books that I recommend, and it's a must-read if you are interested in building wealth.

- $31,367, the average price paid for a car by millionaires

- $41,997, the average price paid for a car by decamillionaires (those with a net worth of $10 million)

- 63% purchase used vehicles

- 81% buy cars and don't lease

- A majority of millionaires have written budgets

If you want to be rich, do what rich people do. The foundation to a solid financial future is the following steps:

1. Get on a written spending plan.

2. Pay off all your debts (except for the house). Yes, get rid of that car payment!

3. Build up an emergency fund of 3 to 6 months' expenses.

4. Work towards investing at least 15% of your income, preferably 20% or more, if your goal is early retirement.

Paying Off Debts

You can listen to my show, *Financial Rock Star*, or visit my website, ScottAlanTurner.com, for information on getting out of debt. Based on my own personal experience with building my own wealth and researching how others built their wealth, a common thread is paying off your high interest debts **first** before you start investing. It makes zero sense to try to invest and earn a 10% rate of return when you have a credit card balance with an 18% interest rate.

Many people have car loans, credit card debt, medical bills, student loans, etc. While it might seem like a good idea to pay down debt and invest at the same time, it often isn't.

You might want to attack from both ends: reducing debt and saving at the same time. There are psychological benefits knowing that you are putting money away for the future. If you must do both, try saving 1% and put all extra money towards reducing debt.

For example if you had credit card debt with a 20% interest rate, paying off the credit is the same as earning a 20% annual (yearly) return. You'll discover later it's not possible (okay, very, very highly unlikely) to find a place where your money will grow 20% annually. Because of that, paying the debt down to zero saves you from paying 20% in interest, so it's the best investment you can make for yourself.

Paying off your debts first is the best use of your money because it has a high guaranteed return. Monthly debt payments can rob you of your retirement or your other savings goals. So clean out that fridge by paying off your debts first.

What you could have if you invested monthly at 10% per year:

Monthly Payment	5 years	10 years	15 years	20 years	25 years
$100	$7,744	$20,485	$41,447	$75,937	$132,683
$200	$15,487	$40,969	$82,894	$151,873	$265,367
$300	$23,231	$61,453	$124,341	$227,810	$398,050
$400	$30,975	$81,938	$165,788	$303,748	$530,733
$500	$38,719	$102,422	$207,235	$379,684	$663,417
$600	$46,462	$122,907	$248,682	$455,621	$796,100
$700	$54,206	$143,391	$290,129	$531,558	$928,783
$800	$61,950	$163,876	$331,576	$607,495	$1,061,467
$900	$69,693	$184,360	$373,023	$683,432	$1,194,150
$1,000	$77,437	$204,845	$414,470	$759,369	$1,326,833
$1,200	$92,924	$245,814	$497,364	$911,243	$1,592,200
$1,500	$116,156	$307,267	$621,705	$1,139,053	$1,990,250
$2,000	$154,874	$409,690	$828,941	$1,518,738	$2,653,667

Your Next Step: If you have debt, please visit my website where I have several articles on strategies to pay off your debts as fast as possible.

Emergency Money

Having an emergency stash of cash equal to 3 to 6 months of expenses is the next step in preparing to invest. While you might think putting money away you'll need in 30 years is a higher priority, having cash to be able to handle a loss of income, medical emergency, or some other situation is important to *staying* out of debt.

After I bought my first house, I was left with an empty bank account and a mortgage payment coming up. As a single person if I had lost my job or become unable to work, I would not have been able to pay my mortgage. There are countless stories of people in this situation—they have no cushion for bad times. Unfortunately, bad things happen. And it becomes much worse when you have little or no income and no money to pay the bills.

Your Next Step: If you don't have an emergency fund, visit my website, ScottAlanTurner.com, and I'll show you how to calculate how much you need and where to put the money.

Got No Money to Invest?

Tracking my spending allows me to see if I'm wasting my money on stuff I don't care about or don't need. I've been doing it for 15 years, and it's such an eye-opener. But what I like about tracking where my money goes is it's allowed me to stockpile money by becoming a more conscious spender. I do not feel deprived. I spend money on the things I love (vacations with my family), and cut costs on unimportant stuff (which to me is eating out for lunch, clothing, cars, and gadgets).

Having a written spending plan to track where your money is going to go each month will free you to take control of your situation.

Your Next Step: Try out my Latte Factor calculator on ScottAlanTurner.com. It will show you what small changes in your life can add up to over time. For example—*how much will skipping one dinner out each week save you over 30 years?*

What if you brought your lunch to work every day and invested the savings?

What if you got rid of your car loan?

It's a real eye-opener as to what our financial decisions cost us over our lifetimes.

I'm not saying you should give up all the treats and frills in your life. We need some rewards for our hard work. However, you need to be aware of where your money goes and understand if you hide a little before you spend it, you can build a healthy retirement nest. How do you hide money? Next you'll discover the secret to saving.

8. Eating Out for Every Meal

Eating out can be very expensive and is one of the big money busters people have in their monthly spending. But what if you had every meal prepared for you, and you never had to cook again in your life? Better yet, every meal was delivered right to your front door (like pizza delivery!)?

You would be automating all your meals.

Another important component of building wealth is the ongoing investment of your income for long periods of time. The best way to do that is through automating your savings.

If you have a company retirement plan like a 401(k) (explained later), you might already be doing this. With every paycheck, money gets taken out and invested in your employer's retirement plan.

If you invest on your own, setting up money to be taken from your paycheck each month automatically is a sure-fire way to keep from spending that money.

You sometimes hear this called "paying yourself first." It's setting aside a piece of your monthly income for your future needs and wants.

A big reason people are so behind on retirement savings is because they spend every dollar they earn (sometimes more) and live paycheck-to-paycheck. The money comes in, and it gets spent. Often on stuff. Or eating out, whatever.

If you have money taken out of your checking/savings account before you can buy stuff or spend it on eating out, you will never miss it. And if it's automatic, you don't have to remember to transfer the money once a month for the next 30 years, which, of course, you would forget to do. Be lazy and automate.

Your Next Step: If you have an employer plan, try setting aside 1% of your salary today to start your investment future. Then in six months, bump it up to 2%. Over time as your income increases through promotions, raises, or bonuses, keep increasing your savings while keeping your cost of living the same.

Whatever your number is, you have to stick to it, all the time. Good times. Bad times. All the time. Why? Because of the power of compounding. Slow, steady savings, for long periods.

More than anything else, the key to building wealth is saving more/spending less than you earn. It's such a simple concept. If you have kids, I suggest you start teaching it to them. If you can spend less than you earn, everything else in life becomes a thousand times simpler.

If you want to achieve your goals in less time, set a goal to save 20% of what you earn. If you can't do that, start by saving 1%. If you can't do that, commit to saving half of every pay raise. Half of every tax return. Half of every bonus.

The more you save, the faster you achieve financial independence. Frugal millennials that saved 70% to 80% of their income in their twenties are now retiring in their thirties.

Overcome your current situation, then commit to automating your savings.

You'll be faced with thousands of different places to put your money and a dizzying array of terms. It's no wonder you might be confused. It can be an endless circle of jargon. Next, I'll walk you through the basic ingredients, measurements, grocery shopping, so you can become a master chef in no time. Let's get cooking . . .

PART 2

Foundations of Investing:

Basic Cooking Skills

9. The Chocolate Caramel Crunchy Clusters Business

Taylor and Kim realize they have a winner on their hands with their Chocolate Caramel Crunchy Clusters.

"Hey," suggests Taylor, "let's start a business!"

And 4C is born.

After brainstorming one night, Kim states, "If we could sell a 100,000 of these, we would be rich!"

"Yes," Taylor replies. "But where can we get the money? And the equipment to make them all? And the bags to store them in?"

Taylor asks his dad, who knows a lot about business, what he should do.

"You need to form a business and find some investors," his dad recommends.

"What's an investor?" Taylor asks.

His dad explains, "An investor is someone who gives a business money in the hopes it will turn that money into more money for them. Business owners often need to raise money, so they can grow their business—hiring people, buying equipment, and office space.

"Say, Rick next door likes your candy, and he gives you $1,000 so that he can become an owner in your company. *Stocks* are shares of ownership in a company. At its simplest, it's a piece of paper called a 'stock certificate' that you can sell to anyone, allowing them to invest their money in your business. People who own stock are called stockholders, shareholders, investors, or owners.

"So this guy Rick is wanting to buy $1,000 worth of stocks in your business because he is hoping you'll sell a lot of candy and grow the business. And that you'll open candy stores all around the city. Or that you'll land a big deal with Walmart or CVS to sell your candy. If Walmart sells your candy, your business is going to be much bigger, right?"

"Yes," Taylor agrees.

"And if the company is bigger, it will be worth more, right?" his father inquires.

"Yes," confirms Taylor.

"Then Rick's share of the company will be worth much more than the $1,000 he originally invested in stocks because your company is worth more."

Investing is putting your money to work for you so that it will earn more money. People are willing to risk their money and invest in a company (by buying *stock* in it) because they hope the company will do well. The investor will be rewarded if the value of the company goes up. If the value of the company goes up, the investor can sell their stock investments to someone else for more than they paid for them, so that's how the investor makes money.

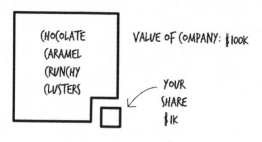

I YEAR LATER

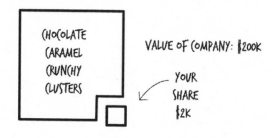

3 YEARS LATER, 3 STORES

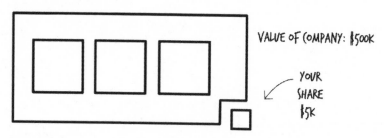

Taylor then asks, "Is there any other way to raise money?"

"Yes," his dad says. "You can issue a *bond*. A bond is a loan you take out where you promise to pay back the loan with interest on a specific date. If you sold Rick a $1,000-bond, you might agree to take his $1,000, pay him 5% a year ($50 a year) for the next ten years, and then repay his $1,000. You used his money for ten years to grow the business, but you had to give him a little money to borrow it."

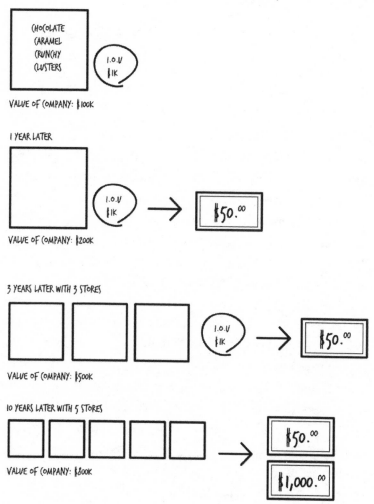

Investing in *stocks* and *bonds* is very common. Now that you can explain the differences between the two, it's time to dig into how to turn that knowledge into more money by staying away from chocolate-covered green beans.

10. The Failure of Chocolate-Covered Green Beans

Say you and I want to earn some extra money. An easy way to do that is to buy a few lemons, some sugar, and set up a lemonade stand on a busy street intersection during the summer. Maybe we buy the ingredients for $20. There's a pretty good chance we're going to sell some lemonade when it's hot out. It's a good "risk." We'll spend some money on the ingredients, sell it for $0.25 a glass, work for a few hours, and make $30. Our profit is $10, so our "rate of return" is 50%.

The following week, you and I are in the kitchen trying to come up with something exotic and tasty that nobody else has ever eaten, or even heard of. We decide on making chocolate-covered green beans (sounds delicious!). They taste decent, so we go out and spend every last dollar we have at all the local grocery stores, buying up all the green beans and chocolate we can find. It costs us $200 for the ingredients. We set up a table again on a hot summer day, and . . . nothing. No sales. We not only don't make money, we lost the $200 we spent.

A good "risk" is something that has a track record that's been proven over time. A bad "risk" is something that is unproven (zero history), no track record (a short history), or has a high degree of uncertainty (too risky).

No Risk, No Money

After getting our butts handed to us on the chocolate-covered green bean fiasco, we go back to the drawing board. This time you and I decide on making some chocolate-and-caramel-covered macadamia nut clusters. But before we can buy the ingredients, we have to mow lawns to save up more money. The day arrives, and we head out to the curb with our goodies. We sell out in an hour, making $70 in profit after spending $35 on ingredients. Our rate of return was 100%.

While we took on another risky venture, there was a little more certainty. Judging by the many candy bars with similar ingredients, people like the combination of chocolate, caramel, and nuts. It was much less risky than chocolate-covered green beans. But we took on greater risk because nobody had ever tasted one before. Everyone knows the flavor of lemonade. Not nearly as many people like green beans.

You're not taking risks just to take risks. There is a reason why you are investing—to make more money than if you just took your cash and hid it in under your mattress. When you take bigger risks, the reward can be not just dreaming about the things you've always desired—but having them.

With virtually all investments, as the risk goes up, so does the return.

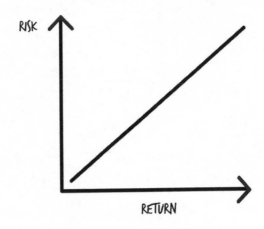

You would probably consider owning a home a good risk.

If you own a home or you plan on owning a home someday, you took a risk or will take one on buying that property. Real estate has a pretty good track record over time of going up in value. It's something a lot of people feel safe investing in. But there is no guarantee with real estate, so you take a risk with buying a home too. For most people, a home is the biggest purchase they will ever make. If you own a home, you're already used to taking risks. Based on looking around your neighborhood, you can see plenty of other people doing the same thing—taking an educated risks based on the history of real estate.

The payment on a home is usually fixed—the mortgage payment. It stays the same for the entire 15, 20, or 30 years you plan on owning the home. During that period, the value of the home goes up. Your risk is the money you put into owning the home. The reward is the value goes up. When you sell the house, it's hopefully worth more than what you paid for it. You make money.

But that doesn't always happen. Home prices can go down. They can go way down. Home prices in a place like Detroit, Michigan, were so bad after the auto industry collapsed between 2008 and 2010, you could buy an entire street of homes for a few thousand dollars.

That's not typical. Real estate is a good, pretty safe investment. If you own a home or are planning on owning one someday, you're open to taking on risk.

- If you buy a home there is risk—the value could go down.

- If you loan your friend $20, there is risk—they might not pay you back.

- If you invest, there is risk—you might lose money.

- If you don't save for retirement, there is risk—of being broke in retirement.

- If you put money in a cookie jar, there is risk. (And not the risk of someone stealing the money.) You run the risk of not keeping up with inflation. That's a big risk.

The bottom line with risk is—you're already taking it. If you're doing something or you're doing nothing, you're taking risks.

Your Next Step: Ask yourself how much risk you are willing to take. Can you handle having a $1,000,000 drop to $500,000, then go back to $1,250,000 over a period of a few years? Take too little risk and you won't earn as much money. Take too much risk, and you could lose all your money (don't worry, if you follow my advice, that won't happen).

Some people don't like to take risks with their investments, but by doing this, you expose yourself to higher risks when you're older—you might run out of money. You can't live without taking risks, but there are proven steps you can take with your investments to reduce your risks while still earning a healthy return. But before you decide on what to do with your money, let's look at the different ways you can hold it.

11. Big Carts, Little Carts, Flat Carts, Kid Carts

At the grocery store you've probably seen all the different types of carts. You've got the regular shopping cart, the bright yellow kids shopping cart that seats two screaming kids because only one has the steering wheel, the hand basket, and for good measure, we'll throw in a giant flatbed cart, like you might see at Costco or Home Depot. But no matter what kind of cart you have, you can put a box of Cheerios in it.

The carts of the investing world are "accounts." Let's call them big containers, like a grocery cart. There are different types of carts, but they generally hold the same stuff. You can think of it like your banking accounts. A checking account and a savings account are different accounts, but they both hold cash.

With investing the different account types (carts) are:

- Company-based plans (401(k), 403(b), 457, Thrift Savings Plan)

- Individual Retirement Account (Traditional IRA or Roth IRA)

- College saving plans (529 College Savings Plan)

- Regular investment account (brokerage account)

Some of the names might sound familiar. There are others, but these are the most common and the ones we'll cover. The primary difference between them is when you pay taxes on the money you put in the account (i.e., invest in the account).

Company-based plans—Plans that let you automatically set aside part of your paycheck towards your retirement. The benefit of these plans is that by contributing part of your paycheck now, you reduce your taxes now. You don't pay taxes until you withdraw the money during retirement. Their strange names come from the sections of the IRS tax code they are based on. 401(k)s are available in many for-profit companies (Coke, Home Depot, maybe even your local grocery store). 403(b) plans are for non-profit companies, like hospitals and schools. 457(b) plans are for government employees. Thrift Savings Plans are for federal employees.

IRAs—IRAs are retirement plans available if you don't have a company plan or if you have contributed the maximum amount allowed to a company retirement plan.

College saving plans—The 529 College Savings Plan is the most popular plan to allow parents and grandparents to invest money and let it grow tax-free and be withdrawn tax-free to pay for higher education.

Regular brokerage account—An investment account with no special tax advantages. You might hear it called a "taxable investment account" or "individual brokerage account."

For each of the different carts, they can all hold the same stuff. Just like the box of Cheerios can fit into any type of shopping cart.

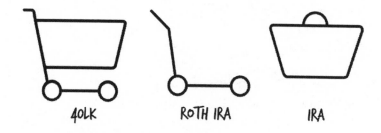

401K   **ROTH IRA**   **IRA**

Your Next Step: If you have one of these accounts, log in now and poke around. Don't make any changes yet! Just take a look if you haven't checked in a while. What do you see?

Most people think a 401(k) is an investment, but it isn't. And a savings account isn't money. You just discovered they are containers until you put something in them. The question you then have to ask is—*What goes in them?* Let's find out . . .

12. What Goes in the Carts?

If you're buying groceries to feed yourself or your family, you'll no doubt be picking up a few different things at the store:

- Entrees (chicken fried steak, lasagna, fried chicken, rotisserie chicken, etc.)

- Side items (mashed taters, tater tots, French fries, maybe a vegetable)

- Bread (Hawaiian rolls, French bread, sour dough bread, dinner rolls)

These are classes of food or different ways to group them, the same as you would find on a menu at a restaurant or in a cookbook.

When it comes to investing, in this book, stocks, bonds, and cash are all types of "assets"—something that has value and is worth something. And stocks, bonds, and cash are the three main types of "asset classes" discussed. An asset class describes **how** similar things behave, which I'll describe next.

Note: There are some other asset classes I'll mention later, but they aren't appropriate for getting started, and many aren't appropriate for experienced investors either.

Stocks

Consider if you and a friend split the cost of an order of 8 chicken strips. You both shared in the cost, and you both own a share of the strips. Each chicken strip would be one share.

Think of stocks (also called "equities") like a main dish on a plate when you eat out. The entree. A perfectly grilled steak. The portion is usually bigger, it takes up a bigger part of the plate, and it's the most expensive part of the dish. If the chef screws up cooking the main dish (it's overcooked), the restaurant loses money if you send it back to the kitchen.

Stocks are like that. The stock asset class has the potential to make or lose a lot of money, so the risk and return are high. When you buy stock, you are buying a small piece of ownership in a company. The return comes as the value of the company goes up. You can buy stock in companies, like McDonald's, Coca-Cola, Facebook, Apple.

When you buy stock, you become a stockholder, shareholder, owner, and investor. Stocks are sold in "shares," because you share in the ownership of the company with other stockholders. You can't eat stock like you can chicken strips though.

Bonds

Bonds are like a side item. They are safer to whip up in the kitchen and harder to mess up. Think mashed potatoes.

Because they are safer as an investment, the returns of bonds are lower (not as tasty as the main dish). A bond is a type of debt where the company owes you money. You can buy bonds from companies, like McDonald's and Coca-Cola, as well as from the government.

High-quality bonds have a lower return than stocks because they are less risky. For example, a local government might sell some bonds to build some new highways. It's rare the government can't pay back its debts to the investors that loaned them the money, so the risk is lower.

Cash

Cash is like a bread roll on your plate. They don't have to be refrigerated and can be tossed in a breadbox. They are easy to prepare, and you can pull one out and immediately start munching on it.

Cash, like rolls, is easily accessed, like the money in your checking account. No cooking or heating required! That's called "liquidity." Liquidity refers to the speed in which an asset can be accessed as cash in case you need it to buy something. Generally for investments that are more liquid, there is less return.

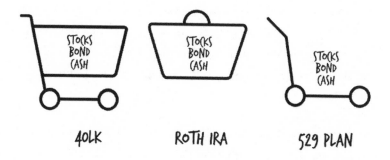

40LK   ROTH IRA   529 PLAN

If you have a bag of rolls, you can take them out and stuff your face. Cash is very liquid. If you own a home, you can't eat the house. You would have to sell it first, which might take eight days or eight months. Real estate is not liquid.

Stocks have the highest return but also the greatest risk to your money.

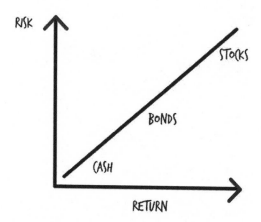

How risky are stocks? During 2007 to 2009 stocks lost 54%[4] of their value. A million dollars in the stock market became $460,000. You might wonder how you would feel about losing that much money, which is why balancing risk and return is important.

Your Next Step: Ask a friend, co-worker, or relative if they have any investments and what percent are stocks vs. bonds. See if they can explain to you why they chose stocks vs. bonds. You'll learn later the reasons for investing in stocks vs. bonds.

Now it should be clear—assets, like stocks, bonds, and cash, get put into containers (401(k)s, IRAs, college savings accounts). So are you ready to find out how you can measure if you're a good investor or not? It's time to head to "the market" and comparison shop.

13. Where Do Groceries Come From?

It's funny that with all these food analogies, there is one you've most likely heard—"the market." The market is like a farmers market. Farmers bring in food to sell at one price, and shoppers buy it at a higher price. Depending on if a particular crop is doing well (a good orange harvest) or poorly (there was a flood, and the peanut crops rotted), the price of a particular food item might vary day to day, week to week, and year to year.

When you flip on the nightly news or read the news online, each day you'll hear, "The market is up" or "The market is down." What is "the market"? What are they talking about?

The "market" is short for "stock market."

It's the market where stocks are bought and sold ("traded").

The names of the two most common measurements of how the market is doing are the S&P 500 and the Dow Jones Industrial Average (the Dow).

The S&P 500 is a list of the 500 largest companies in America (this is not 100% accurate but close enough for what you need to know).

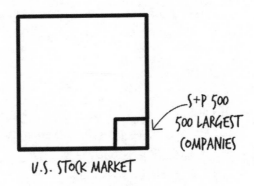

S+P 500
500 LARGEST
COMPANIES

U.S. STOCK MARKET

The Dow is a mix of 30 big companies that represent the overall stock market. The Dow includes companies, like Disney, Microsoft, Exxon, and General Electric.

While there are thousands of companies in the stock market, the Dow and S&P 500 are used to represent the overall market. Think of it like taking a survey of 500 people, instead of surveying the entire population. The survey of the 500 gives you an idea of what the whole population is doing.

The companies included in the Dow and the S&P 500 are looked at each day and then compared to what happened the previous day. Is the market up, or is it down from yesterday? Also, the results are looked at for the current year: is the market up or down this year compared to last year, the past 5 years, and so on?

The 2,000-Calorie-Per-Day, Average Person

On the back of packaged food items, you'll find the nutritional info, comparing the vitamins and contents to a 2,000-calorie-per-day, average diet. If you eat a little fewer calories than the assumed 2,000, you'll lose weight. Eat a little more, and you'll gain weight.

The S&P 500 is the gauge, the benchmark, the yardstick, that other investments are compared against. It's the average, like the 2,000-calorie-per-day diet. Historically from 1926 to the present, the S&P 500 has returned a little over 10% a year. Some years it might go up 25%. Some years it might go down 25%. But over a long period, the return averages 10%.[5]

If you earn a lower return, you'll make less money than the S&P average. If you earn a higher return, you can make more money than the S&P average. Just like eating more or fewer calories.

The average annual rate of return of the S&P 500 is often used to make investing choices and to compare one investment to another.

What Makes the Market Go Up or Down?

Market ups and downs are often driven by emotions—how someone, some group, or even an analyst feels about something.

- A CEO gets fired. Now the company has to find a new captain to sail the ship.
- Oprah invests in a company, and suddenly the company is more valuable.

- The cost of materials goes up, causing profits to go down.
- Just in time for Christmas is the hot new toy this year, which stores can't keep on shelves.
- A revolutionary new product is developed that will change the world.
- New government regulations are going to negatively impact the company.
- The company announces it will lay off 20% of its employees.

It's very unpredictable, though billions of dollars are spent each year *trying* to predict it.

In 2008 to 2009 the market dropped 54% over an 18-month period. What happened after that? Over the next 5 years the market tripled in value. Nearly every time after the stock market drops significantly, it recovers in an average of 12 months.

In the history of the stock market, as measured by the S&P 500, if you look at any 20-year period, the market has *never* lost money.

Your Next Step: Check the business section of "Google News" and look at the headlines. See how many different reasons you can find for the market going up or down yesterday.

You might think all you need to do is just invest in "the market," and you can safely let your money compound at 10% a year. If that were the whole story, the book would be over, but there is more to creating an income for life. It's time to turn the page and learn what so many others fail to do.

14. Donuts—Is There Anything They Can't Do?

Say you had a friend named Julia who created a brand-new food invention, which she's calling the Choconut. It's a fluffy donut made of chocolate. You think the Choconut is going to be the next Cinnabon, so you invest every penny you own in Julia's new business.

The first few years Choconut shops are opening up on every street corner in town. Everything looks great, and it looks like your investment was a great choice. Until one day Julia declares bankruptcy and has to close down all the stores. It turns out Julia was a great cook but didn't know how to run a business, so she ran out of money to pay bills.

You lose all the money you invested, and now you're broke. While there was a possibility of earning a lot of money, you lost all your money because you weren't **diversified**. The "return" was high, but it came with a lot of "risk."

You may have heard the saying, **"Don't put all your eggs in one basket."** Because if you drop the one basket, you break all the eggs.

If you put all your hope in one business and the business fails, you've lost everything. How do we avoid that?

Buying Several Donut Businesses

What if instead of investing in just Choconuts, you had also invested in Krispy Kreme, Dunkin Donuts, and Voodoo Doughnuts?

You "spread" your money around evenly to different donut shops. You diversified a little more. Your "risk" is "lower."

It's certainly an improvement. Even though Choconuts is out of business, you only lost some of your money. The other donut shops are still in business.

The Donut Outlaws

What if the imperial federal government comes along and issues a law, stating, "Donuts are causing children to get poor grades in schools. All donut shops will be outlawed for the sake of the children."

Forget about the uproar that would be caused by the loss of donuts to our society and our ability to carry on; if you had only invested in donut shops, you would lose all your money.

Even though you were more diversified, you weren't diversified enough to reduce the risk of losing some or all of your investment.

Buy More Food and Everything Else Too

To diversify for your health, you need to eat food from all kinds of different food groups.

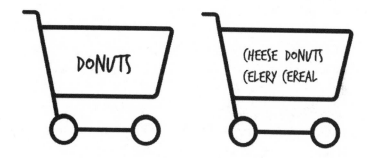

To maintain financial health, you need to diversify where you put your money—where you invest. The money needs to be spread around to reduce risk. How do you do that?

You would buy a little of everything from all different kinds of companies:

- Retail (The Gap, Foot Locker, Macy's)
- Energy (Exxon, Shell, BP)
- Banks (Bank of America, Wells Fargo)
- Technology (Microsoft, Apple, Facebook)
- Airlines (Delta, American, Southwest)
- Home improvement (Home Depot, Lowes)
- Food (Walmart, Kroger, Publix)
- And, of course, donuts (Dunkin Donuts, Krispy Kreme)

Swiss Chocolate

If donuts get outlawed in the US because of trans fats, you could still get your sweets from elsewhere in the world. You can have French pastries, Swiss chocolate, Greek baklava.

Your investing plan should include some international companies too. Often when the American economy is down, somewhere else in the world, a country's economy is up. For example, Japan might be doing well when the US is not. Or vice versa. It's rarely the case that the entire world economy is down (but it can happen).

By spreading your money around in both domestic *and* international companies, you're further diversifying, and it's **one more way to reduce risk.** And you want to reduce risk while still getting a good return, right? Thankfully, you have access to massive diversification. Let's look at how you can get it.

15. The Food Buffets of the World

To get the ultimate in diversity in eating, what would you need to buy? One of *every* food item at the grocery store. You buy a box of Wheaties, a bag of Kettle chips, bananas, Ben & Jerry's ice cream, some bagels, maybe some more Ben & Jerry's ice cream, etc.

When you think about all the things a grocery store sells, you realize that could cost you thousands of dollars. Even buying a few dozen things can cost hundreds of dollars on your grocery bill.

But what about if you go out to the all-you-can-eat buffet? Ryans or Golden Corral? Then you just pay the $11.99 or whatever it costs to get a taste of everything. There are hundreds of choices at the buffet, and you are able to pay to get a little of everything for a low cost. The price you pay—your money—gets spread out amongst all the different dishes that you didn't have to buy individually from the grocery store.

- Parmesan chicken
- fried chicken
- scrambled eggs
- sausage
- donuts
- chicken fingers
- shrimp and chicken
- sautéed chicken
- donuts

- chocolate chip cookies
- carrot cake
- vanilla ice cream
- cornbread
- donuts
- brownies
- maybe a salad

Remember, if we were going to the grocery store and buying 200 individual items, it would cost hundreds and hundreds of dollars. Likewise, if you were to buy all 500 individual stocks from the companies in the S&P 500 list, it would cost *tens of thousands of dollars*.

But if you go buffet-style and head over to Ryans or Golden Corral and put down your $11.99, you get access to hundreds of food choices. You get a little bit of everything.

How can they do that?

It's because so many other people—probably 1,000 every day—are also paying $11.99 each. The food can be purchased at a low cost because of the buying power of the group. Individually you would pay a fortune to buy all the ingredients and make 100 different entrees, side dishes, and desserts. Collectively—"mutually"—a big group of people can do it together, so everyone can afford it.

Everyone going to the restaurant has mutually funded, mutually paid for, the food buffet, so everyone can have a little taste of everything.

A "mutual fund" is a type of investment that works the same way. When you buy a mutual fund, you buy a bunch of companies all at once that you wouldn't otherwise be able to afford on your own. When you buy a mutual fund—say for $15.99—you own a tiny, tiny sliver of several dozen, or more often, several hundred, companies. Just like buying at the buffet.

People come together and pool their money, and they mutually agree to fund the purchase of a group of stocks. That's it. That's how a mutual fund works. Everyone gets a little piece of ownership in the companies purchased by the person managing the fund. The person managing the fund is called the—you guessed it—"fund manager."

Mutual funds are awesome because you can buy so many companies at a low cost. Mutual funds have built-in diversification, which lowers your risk.

The primary way you make money with mutual funds or stocks is to buy a share at one price—$25.00 for example—hold it for a long period of time, and sell it for a profit—$200.00, for example. There are other ways mutual funds make money, but I'm not going to overwhelm you with that information in this book.

But I Like Mexican Food

Are there different kinds of buffets out there? Yes, there are. Breakfast buffets, Chinese buffets, Mexican buffets, pizza buffets, and my all-time favorite—all-you-can-eat meat buffets at Texas de Brazil.

Just as there are different kinds of food buffets, there are different kinds of mutual funds. You can tell what type of food (or companies) is in a mutual fund by the name of the fund.

- A *domestic stock* mutual fund invests only in stock from US companies.

- A *domestic bond* mutual fund invests only in bonds from US companies.

- An *international stock* mutual fund invests in stocks from non-US companies.

- A *global stock* mutual fund invests in stocks from both US and non-US companies.

Here are some other common names used to describe mutual funds:

- *Growth*—stocks that have the potential to grow faster than the market

- *Aggressive Growth*—small companies that are growing quickly. These funds have high volatility (they can experience big gains and losses).

- *Growth + Income*—a fund that includes companies that are growing and companies that make payouts to investors each year

- *Balanced*—a lower-risk fund of stocks and bonds that aims for stability

Note: I included the names above (growth, balanced, etc.) because you might come across them. They have nothing to do with the strategies outlined in this book. I mention them just so you're aware of them and because some people claim it's the best way to invest. They aren't, which you will discover as you read on.

You become even more diversified (and further reduce your risk) when you buy several different types of mutual funds. You might want a fruit mutual fund, a dairy mutual fund, a protein mutual fund, and a vegetable mutual fund. On top of those, you might pick an international fruit fund in case a freeze or flood destroys the orange and lemon trees in Florida one spring.

Your Next Step: Explain to someone what a mutual fund is and how it works. Why? Because one of the best ways for you to learn and remember is by teaching someone else these valuable lessons.

Diversification is where it's at. And mutual funds provide simple diversification for all. However, there are thousands of mutual funds to pick from, and mutual funds have a dark side, which is why you need to understand a vastly superior investment that we'll cover next.

16. Buying a Piece of Every Fruit

If you took a notepad and wrote down every type of fruit on the planet, you would have created a Total Fruit Index.

Total Fruit Index: Apple, Apricot, Avocado, Abiu, Acai, Acerola, Ackee, Arhat, American Mayapple, African Cherry Orange, Amazon Grape, Araza . . .

An "index" is just a list of stocks or bonds someone decided to group together. I mentioned the S&P 500 as the market benchmark. It's a list of the 500 biggest companies in the US stock market.

An "index fund" is a type of mutual fund. You will hear it called an "index mutual fund," an "index fund," or even an "index."

*Note: An index fund is a type of mutual fund. A mutual fund is not an index fund. When you see the term "mutual fund" tossed around, it does **not** refer to an index fund. You'll know if you're reading or hearing about an index fund if it has the word "INDEX" in the name. If it doesn't, it's a mutual fund, not an index fund.*

An S&P 500 Index fund is a fund that contains the 500 stocks in the S&P 500 Index. Easy right? The S&P 500 Index fund is considered part of the stock asset class, because it contains stocks of many companies. Mutual funds that contain stocks are also part of the stock asset class. There is no index fund asset class, or mutual fund asset class. Just stocks, bonds, and cash. There are also bond index funds, which would fall under the bond asset class.

Exchange-Traded Funds—ETFs

The more advanced investors and financial planners would get on me if I didn't at least mention exchange traded funds (ETFs). An ETF is basically a mutual fund that you can buy and sell like a stock. They have some features that appeal to some investors. My opinion is they amount to information overload and may cause overwhelm when considering part 5: "What Do I Invest In?" For those reasons, I'm not covering ETFs in this book.

Your Next Step: If you have an employer retirement plan, check your account to see if you have any index funds to pick from (don't make any changes yet!).

An index fund has some significant differences that are key to building your wealth compared to a mutual fund (that's not an index fund). The use of index funds is core to the investing strategy of this book. Now that you know the different types of building blocks you can use to cook a meal with, let's describe an eating plan that will have you running marathons until you're 100.

Prospectus—The Nutritional Information of Index and Mutual Funds

Every index fund and mutual fund has a "prospectus"—a document describing the fund. It's like the nutritional information on the side of a box of cereal. It tells you the ingredients and the nutritional information.

People who sell investments love a mutual fund's prospectus—because it adds incredible confusion to you so that you'll rely on their expertise and not your own. One popular mutual fund discussed every week on the radio has a prospectus 41 pages long! It would take you 3 to 4 hours to read it, and you wouldn't understand any of it. It's like going into a Russian grocery store and trying to figure out what to buy. You can't.

When you invest, you'll receive the prospectus for your investments every year—it's required by law. You might get them in the mail or electronically.

There are two important numbers in the prospectus that you should care about:

1. The annual rate of return. It will appear in 1-year, 3-year, 5-year, 10-year, and lifetime percentages.
2. The annual fee. How much you pay each year for the investment. Fees are covered in chapter 23.

Once you're off and running investing after following the steps in this book, you can do what I do every year when you receive a prospectus—ignore the email and delete it, or if it arrives in the mail, walk it from the mailbox to the recycle bin or trashcan.

There is a lot of conflicting advice about your money and what you should do with it. In the next two parts, I'll explain the most common ways people lose money investing and how to avoid them, so you can retire rich. By understanding the most common ways people **lose money** when they invest, you can avoid the same *pitfalls* and instead—**profit**. Let's go . . .

PART 3

Becoming a Successful Investor:

Selecting the Freshest, Highest-quality

Ingredients at the Lowest Cost

17. Would You Eat Cow Stomach?

A man has got to know his limitations.

—Clint Eastwood

In my high school years, my dad walked up to me in the living room and said, "Here, try this," handing me some white-looking stuff. I asked, "What is it?" He replied, "Just try it." I did, and it was disgusting. It turns out it was something called tripe, the stomach lining of a cow. People eat that stuff, and you can buy it at the grocery store. I don't eat food anymore without knowing what it is. And I follow this same principle for investing too. But wait—let me tell you how I got to this point.

My father-in-law used to trade (buy and sell) gold commodities (a type of investment we won't be discussing). At his recommendation Katie wanted to get in on it, so we handed over $8,000 to his broker for some commodities trading. I was against it, but $8,000 wasn't going to sink the retirement ship, so I relented.

Anytime we bought or sold some gold or oil options, it cost us $150. You read that right—$150. Occasionally Katie would get a call with a recommendation from the broker on something we should buy or sell.

After a year and a half, our $8,000 investment was worth $6,500. All of the $1,500 we lost were due to the fees paid to the broker.

I didn't understand commodities, and it's something we should have never done. But because Katie's dad *sometimes* did well, the reasoning was simple—we should get in on it because we could do well too, right?

Never invest in something you can't explain to a high school student, and never invest in something just because your neighbor/co-worker/sister/friend's brother's uncle's second cousin's auto mechanic says he's got a sure-fire investment.

When you see and hear the masses flocking to an investment, it's too late. The money has been made. Don't chase the "hot stock" pick. Don't get caught in the hype pumped out on the front of various money magazines.

You should spend at least as much time studying a particular investment as you do earning the money to put into that particular investment.

—Brian Tracy

The biggest mistake people make when it comes to investing is not understanding what they are investing in.

Think about the types of investments you've heard about on the news (gold?), in magazines (energy companies?), or learned about from a wise old uncle (stamps?). Do you know enough about them to invest in them?

KISS—Keep It Simple, Stupid

I've become what I call a boring investor. I used to be very active in my investments—getting in and out of them, trying to speculate on who would win, trying exotic things outside of the mainstream, run-of-the-mill stuff. Those choices are where I experienced my greatest losses in my finances. I did those things before I became a **smart** investor.

Smart = Boring

I decided I would rather spend my time on anything but investing. I just wanted to pick something that had a proven rate of return, without a lot of risk, that I didn't have to pay much attention to.

Simplicity can often beat out fancier advice when it comes to your money. I could have kept going on and on in this book, doubling its size. But I'm intentionally avoiding information overload because a) it's unnecessary and b) you just need to take action and get started and succeed. If I had a 100-step plan, you would never follow it. That's why it's just simple steps with a lot of material explaining why.

Your Next Step: Decide if you want to try to be a full-time investor or if you would rather spend your time doing other things.

Simple investing simply wins out over complexity. But the real wealth killer isn't lack of knowledge, it's the limiting belief of fear.

If there is anything that can overcome fear, it's a proven history of the market. Learn from history and experiences, and use them to conquer your fears.

18. Oh No—Mad Cow and E. Coli!

Like our food supply, the economy is very resilient.

After 9/11, the worst ever terrorist attacks on American soil, the situation was so dire the government decided to shut down the markets for several days out of fear the market would collapse. Wall Street was right next to the Twin Towers after all.

It was all over the news before the markets opened back up. People were wondering how much of a free fall the economy would take. Everyone was scared. Well, they were right. The market lost 7% of its value when it opened back up.[6] People were in a panic.

What you didn't hear was, fifty-three days later, the market regained everything it had lost. If you had money invested before 9/11 and not touched it for 53 days, you would have never noticed.

What about during 2008 to 2009 when the market lost 54% of its value over 18 months? If you were getting ready to retire and you had $1M, eighteen months later you had $500,000 or worse, if you had invested poorly. That's a big difference. If you had chickened out and decided, "I don't want to be an investor anymore," you missed making all your money back 18 months later.

"But Scott—my parents/neighbors/friends lost their entire 401(k)s during that time!"

And I bet I know why, which we'll cover in this section.

Over the history of the stock market, 1926 to today, if you look at any 10-year period, for example, 2000 to 2010 or 1994 to 2004, the market lost money four times. Ninety-five percent of any 10-year period it went up! That's important because when you invest, it should be for the long term, over a period of decades, to take advantage of compounding.

Fear is a wealth killer. When I start reading about an upcoming market collapse or how the market has dropped significantly in the daily news, I laugh and then skip ahead to the entertainment section to see what the Kardashians are up to (not really).

However, there are no guarantees.

"What? Didn't you just say the economy is resilient? And, wait, you said the average rate of return over time is 10%!"

While those things hold true for the past, no single person, company, advisor, university professor—nobody—has a crystal ball. Yes, some people claim to. And some people might have been right once or twice in the past with their predictions. But even a blind dog finds a bone once in a while . . .

Your Next Step: Think about your risk tolerance. If the market loses 50% tomorrow, will you break out in cold sweat and lose your mind? Or will you shrug it off because you've chosen a proven, winning investment strategy that minimizes your risk while maximizing your return?

Investments can change in value every day. But based on the research I've read, I'm a firm believer in the power of the economy over time and the documented returns of the economy over time. Turn the page to discover why every day is not a good day with your money, and that's okay.

19. Living in Happyland, in a Gumdrop House on Lollipop Lane

One of the best days of my life was when my twins were born. They were so tiny! And one of the worst was when my dad passed away. I miss his gardening tips.

In life, you will agree—some days are great (a fun night out with friends), and some days are not as great (you argue with someone). Some years you look back at all the wonderful things that happened, and some years you want to cry because somebody was really sick or maybe passed away.

Investing is a bumpy ride. Some days your investments are worth more, other days they are worth less. Some years your investments are worth more, and some years your investments are worth less. It's just a fact—and you have to get used to it.

What you *choose* to do during the down-times **and** the up-times has a *significant* impact on your long-term wealth. The time to be in the market is to be in the market all the time.

"I want to start off investing $100 dollars, but would I be making real money in less then a month? I really need to know."

A viewer on my YouTube channel left that comment on one of my investing videos.

I couldn't convince the person that investing is for the long term—5 years or more. Or more appropriately, for a period of decades, so your money can compound. This person wanted to see their money grow *now*. They wanted their gumdrop house on Lollipop Lane in Happyland *now*.

If you want to double your money in a month, go to Vegas and play blackjack or the slot machines.

If you want to build real wealth, you need to know it will take a decade or more of saving and investing. It's a marathon, not a sprint. Anyone that says otherwise is blowing smoke up your skirt. The tortoise beats the hare every time.

The quickest way to get rich is not to get rich quick.

Your Next Step: Be honest with yourself and see if you expect your investments to grow by huge amounts over just a few years' time. Remember, the power of compounding doesn't come in the first few years. It comes much later. Check back to chapter 3 on the magic penny.

You're becoming an investing expert. Choose right now to stay the course and not let the nightly news scare you and incite you to make foolish decisions. Once you set a destination, keep heading towards it, rain or shine. Let's start with how you'll get there much more quickly on the slow one-lane road.

20. New and Improved Flavors vs. Plain Ol' Vanilla

Anne and Paula are identical twins. Paula goes to the gym three times a week in the morning and walks on the treadmill for 45 minutes. She eats the same four meals every day: oatmeal and scrambled eggs for breakfast; grilled chicken, brown rice, and mixed vegetables for lunch; a PB&J sandwich with a banana for an afternoon snack; and baked fish with a salad for dinner. Day after day, this is what she eats. *Year after year.* She has the most *boring* diet in the world but follows it consistently. The result is she is fit as a fiddle. She doesn't have to work hard to maintain her girlish figure, never has to get ready for swimsuit season by crash dieting, and always has lots of energy. She eats the occasional chocolate chip cookie or a bowl of ice cream in moderation to stay energized, and she feels good about her results.

Anne is the exact opposite. Anne loves to eat and party. Anne is a yo-yo dieter, and her weight goes up and down, 10 to 50 pounds every year. Some years she looks like a runway model and other years like she could be a linebacker for the Chicago Bears football team. Anne tries the Paleo diet (no carbs) for a while, then she might switch to juicing for a few months, back to Paleo, then to a strict vegan diet, and many times the seafood diet—if she sees food, she eats it. Whatever diet is the latest craze she usually tries it for a while, gets a few quick results, and then rebounds to where she started because of bad eating habits. Some weeks she might lift weights in the gym every day; other times she does spin class for 2 hours a day. Anne buys multiple gym memberships, personal training sessions, and DVDs. Sometimes she does CrossFit and trains for half-marathons. Anne is very active in trying different things to try to maintain a consistent weight, but she ends up failing over and over again. And she nearly always is worse off than her twin sister, Paula.

Paula learned long ago that if she just has a passive plan and does things consistently over time, her simple strategy, while boring, gives her terrific and consistent results. She stays healthy, rarely gets sick, and you would expect her to potentially live a long, active life.

Anne's strategy is constantly changing as she is always trying the latest thing. She is very active in the latest fads. Her results are lousy and inconsistent. Anne is trying to eat everything she wants and go on fad diets to try to beat her sister's boring diet.

And so it is with investing. There is *passive* investing, which uses passively managed, boring index funds that get good results year after year, when measured over decades of time.

And there is *active* (hyper-active even) investing, with actively managed mutual funds. Sometimes they look great in the mirror for a while, only to end up failing to look as good as the boring passive funds in the long run.

Who do you want to be? Active Anne or Passive Paula? Coming up, I'll explain why a boring, passive strategy using index funds makes you more money. But not just a little more, a lot more. Let's see how!

21. The 5-Star Restaurant That's Serving Dog Food

What if I told you the Paleo diet had been around for forty years, and *everyone* that followed the Paleo diet looked great? Would you bother trying another diet? You wouldn't because forty years of history is a pretty good amount of data. If the Dashing Dave Diet had been around for five years and Dave boasted his diet would make you look even better, but you had to spend more money to look better, would you buy into this new diet? It probably depends on how good of a salesperson Dave is to convince you his diet is better than anything else.

In 1974, a guy by the name of John Bogle found after doing some research that the market averaged over time 10%. You've heard that already, right? The market has averaged 10% since 1926 to the present. That's the benchmark.

Bogle decided, "Ten percent is a pretty good return—I'll take it!" All you needed to get a 10% return was to buy the same stocks in the same percentages as found in the S&P 500 Index. Simple. Boring. Passive. But it works.

In other words—here's a list of fruit. Let's just buy what's on the list and eat it. We know we're going to be healthier because of it. We're not going to try to figure out the fruit of the month or the best fruits to eat in 2016. Because, as you know, one year everyone is saying bananas are good for you, and the next scientists tell us bananas have too much sugar. Followed by next year when they tell us something different—drink pomegranate juice instead! No—make that apple juice!

What Bogle also found out—and this is the kicker—is that all of the other active mutual fund managers—those chefs who were putting together buffets—were trying to get a better return than 10% to beat the market average. They were trying to get an 11% return. A 12% return. A 15% return.

Bigger return, more money, right? To get better returns the chefs had to actively spend their time putting together better recipes. And if they could put together a tastier meal, they could charge people more for their buffet. In return the customers would get better-tasting food.

The active managers were looking for the next big thing. The diamond in the rough. Like Active Anne, they were trying to find the next fad diet and quick-fix workout routine that would give them a long and healthy life. The fund managers were looking for that edge to beat that 10% because who wouldn't want to make more than 10%?

But Bogle's research showed—they couldn't do it *consistently* over time. In fact, they were failing miserably. They failed to do it prior to 1974, and they continue to fail to do it today. The active managers thought they were smarter than everyone else, but it turns out they weren't—and aren't. And for those times when an active manager did beat the market, it was a matter of luck.[7]

The chefs, for as much time as they spent in the kitchen whipping up different types of buffets and coming up with "better food," averaged only 8%[8] while the market on its own averaged 10%. On top of that, it was very, very expensive for patrons (investors) to pay chefs every year. Seems like there's people out there paying a lot of money just to eat "plat du dog food" at the fanciest place in town . . .

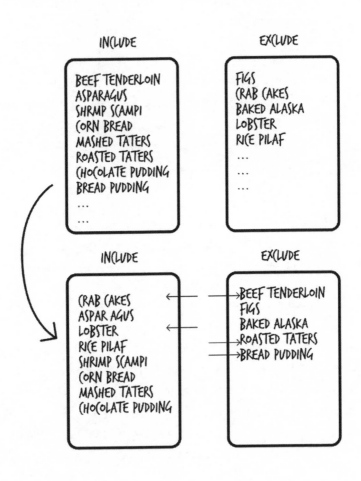

For any given timeframe of a day, week, month, year, even 5 years, an active manager can have better-than-average returns. Over decades though, it doesn't work. Anyone who tells you they can beat the market over time is beating you out of your money.

On average eight of the top 100 funds are in the top 100 funds the following year, as the following chart shows us.[9] How will you know which ones to pick? You have less than an 8% chance year to year.

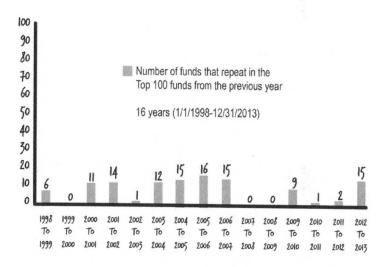

There are professional investors that do this stuff day in and day out for years, and STILL lose money. How can you or I, doing this part-time, expect to do better than they can? What secret knowledge do you have that they don't?

Professionals can't pick winners. A study of the performance of 2,076 professional mutual fund managers over a 32-year time period, from 1975 to 2006, found 99.4% of these managers displayed no evidence of genuine stock-picking skill, and the 0.6% of managers who did outperform the index were "statistically indistinguishable from zero."[10]

The number of funds that have beaten the market over their entire histories is so small that those managers in the 0.6% just got lucky.

What do you think of the investing knowledge of the person you might turn to for advice? Can they pick the best funds every year for decades? Now that you know the professionals are really a bunch of losers, I'll show you how to be a winner and beat them.

22. Low-Cost, Well-Diversified Meals

Live long and prosper.

—Mr. Spock, First Officer, USS Enterprise (Star Trek)

Armed with that information, Bogle created the first **index fund for investors** to match the S&P 500. The fund included all of the stocks listed in the S&P 500.

Bogle called this "being the market." He wasn't trying to *beat* the market because **nobody** was able to do it consistently over time—he aimed simply to *be* the market.

When you start digging into the menus of the restaurants (i.e., the marketing brochures and reports of the mutual funds), you might find they show a better return than 10% some of the time. Maybe for 5 years. Maybe even 10 or 15 years. But that is only part of the story, and if you quit right there, it will cost you.

Buying index funds is a passive investment strategy. Like Passive Paula, we're going to have a boring diet, but it works and is proven.

Note: *In the appendix you will find a bunch of references to studies showing how passive, low-cost index funds make you more money than actively managed funds. I'm not going to bore you by regurgitating the research though I encourage you to look at it, instead of taking me at my word.*

Why pay for an actively managed mutual fund when it doesn't beat the returns of a passively managed index fund?

Many investors want to believe they have found an active fund or superstar fund manager that can beat the market. They think they can do this by looking at the past results of a mutual fund. But what happened yesterday doesn't predict what will happen tomorrow. Advertisers love to use the past returns of a mutual fund to get you to part with your money. Again, the research shows that over time picking actively managed funds based on their past histories will cost you money—and a lot of it.

When you buy individual stocks, it's like buying ten blue M&Ms. You suffer from lack of diversification.

Having an active manager who tries to beat the market and manage a mutual fund is like hiring someone for thousands of dollars to go to the candy store and buy M&Ms in the color and quantity they think is best for you. It has a very high cost.

Buying index funds that are passively managed is like ordering a few cases of M&Ms online in all different colors. It's cheap for you, and you still get a bunch of candy. It's low-cost and proven to have a better return than that of an active manager.

Let's recap—the first big problem with active investing is that 95% of the time the fund managers fail to achieve even the market average in returns. A passive investing strategy will always earn 10% if you buy an index mutual fund that mirrors the S&P 500 Index because the fund **is identical to what is in the S&P 500 Index.** But underperforming the average is just the start of your losing money with these so-called active investing rock stars. It gets much worse.

23. How Much Is It to Run a Kitchen?

Just like a restaurant has operating expenses to keep it running—electricity to keep the lights on, water for dishwashing, employee wages—index and mutual funds also have expenses to keep them running.

These yearly expenses are called—you guessed it—"annual operating expenses." If you buy a mutual fund, you pay these expenses every year. You'll never write a check though; the money is taken out of the fund automatically by the fund managers.

Gordon Ramsey and Mario Batali Don't Come Cheap

If a buffet opened up down the street from your house and Gordon Ramsey or Mario Batali (two famous celebrity chefs) were making the food, would the buffet cost more or less than if I were cooking the food? I make a great hamburger, but you're going to pay more if Gordon is running the restaurant.

What if you're on the Star Trek Enterprise and there is a food replicator?

Okay, if you don't watch Star Trek, replicators are machines in the future where you tell the computer what you want to eat and it appears out of thin air, hot (or cold) and ready-to-eat.

If there is nobody needed to prepare the food, will the buffet cost more or less than if Gordon or Mario is cooking? You got that right—*less*.

The annual fees of having a food replicator are much cheaper than the cost of having Gordon or Mario cooking. There are still some operating costs, but not nearly as much.

Index funds are like food replicators and vending machines—cheap.

Let's take an example index mutual fund that costs you 0.05% each year in fees (you pay 0.05% of your investment balance as the cost each year of investing in the fund).

Now on this next point, the averages are all over the place depending on what study you read and who published the study. The average fee to buy into a restaurant owned by Gordon or Mario—or a mutual fund that is actively managed by a professional fund manager—is around 1.5% yearly. Some data shows 1.2%, some articles use a number as high as 3.17%.[11]

At first glance, it doesn't sound like a big difference. And the chefs would love for you to keep thinking that way because that keeps money in their pockets. But remember compound interest?

Let's compare four different mutual funds in which the only difference is the yearly fees. We use our benchmark average annual return of 10%. What happens to your retirement money if you invest $200 a month for 30 years in each fund? Subtracting out the different example expenses each year, see what happens to your money:

Fund A 10% − 0.05%

Fund B 10% − 0.80%

Fund C 10% − 1.5%

Fund D 10% − 3.17%

Yearly Fees Rob You of Your Retirement!

Fund Name	Yearly Expense Rate	Fund Balance	Effect of Fees
Fund A	0.05%	$408,237	$4,332
Fund B	0.80%	$348,990	$63,578
Fund C	1.5%	$302,279	$110,290
Fund D	3.17%	$216,941	$195,628

Your retirement options are vastly improved if you keep that money in your pocket that would otherwise be paid in fees.

Wow! What a difference over time!

I want to be abundantly clear—the difference in fees can be if you fund your own retirement or you're funding someone else's (the chef's!)

Fees are a wealth killer. They can destroy your retirement and make the difference between eating steak and lobster every week, or living on PB&J.

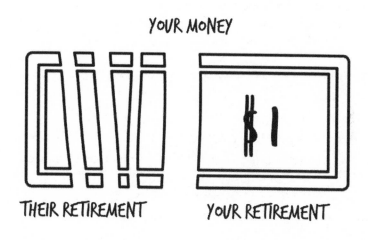

Most 401(k) plans have some of the highest fees you can find. The reason is because employers often pick the cheapest 401(k) plan provider (because it saves the company money). But it costs you money.

Vanguard is the leader in low-fee index funds. You can consider them the Walmart of the investing world. Vanguard was founded by John Bogle in 1974. I mentioned him in chapter 21 as the guy who found that to "be the market" is superior to trying to "beat the market." Other low-cost brokerages are Fidelity, Schwab, and TD Ameritrade. I have been an investor with all four of those companies since 2000.

> Why have I switched over the years? Lower fees. Vanguard is the only company to be owned by the shareholders of the mutual funds. It's like a co-op or credit union, which is owned by the customers. Because shareholders own Vanguard, they have no reason to charge you high fees or have hidden expenses. Currently it costs 0.05% each year to buy into Vanguard S&P 500 Index Fund Admiral Shares ("Fund A" in the previous table).[12]

Your Next Step: If you have a company-sponsored retirement plan, stop reading right now and log in to your account. Check what investments you're in and what some of the fees are. Are they high? Low (less than 0.50%)? Discuss the fees with your co-workers and see if they are aware of how much fees cost them.

The second big problem with active investing is it costs **a lot more** than passive investing. It costs a lot more to hire a celebrity chef to run your restaurant than if you had an automated food replicator or vending machine. Food replicators and vending machines don't get paid million-dollar salaries.

Not only do actively managed funds fail to be the market, you're charged a lot of money on top of that for the privilege of making less money! Talk about adding insult to injury. I will show you the better way, so you line your pockets and not someone else's, but first you have to make **the** most important decision regarding your investments.

24. Creating a Balanced Meal Plan for a Long, Healthy Life

As a child, I grew up eating a lot of sandwiches, sugary cereals for breakfast, and TV dinners. As I've aged, I can't eat some foods I used to be able to because they make me feel lousy.

The "allocation" of the food groups you could eat at a younger age shifts over time as you age and your body changes. A 60-year-old man is at a greater risk of having heart disease compared to a 15-year-old, right? They have different diets and foods they should eat.

Your risk goes up for your health over time, so it's important to focus more on your food choices as you age.

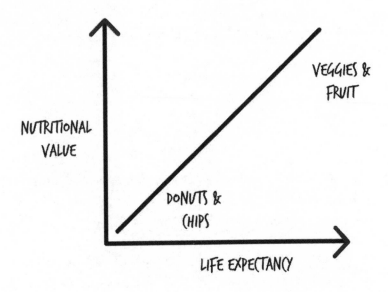

In chapter 12, we talked about the three main asset classes—stocks, bonds, and cash. When it comes to being a smart investor, how you allocate your money between these three things is super important, just like the importance of the foods you eat as you age if you want to live longer and feel better.

It's called "asset allocation." It's the fancy way of describing the breakdown of groceries in your shopping cart. Asset allocation is **the most important decision** you will make regarding your investments. It's more important than any single investment you're going to make in stocks or bonds. It's even more important than choosing index funds over actively managed mutual funds, which we'll get back to repeatedly in upcoming chapters.

- Allocate incorrectly, and you'll have a financial heart attack—you'll run out of money before you run out of life.

- Allocate properly, and you can leave hundreds of thousands of dollars to your kids and grandkids.

- Allocate incorrectly, and you'll be sweating the huge market swings and have sleepless nights.

- Allocate properly, and you'll sleep like a baby, no matter what the market is doing, even if there is a giant earthquake, an outbreak of war, a real estate market collapse, or an alien invasion (maybe not an alien invasion).

When you're young, you can load up on meat, potatoes, and desserts. It's less of a risk because you have decades ahead of you (assuming you aren't a complete couch potato). When you invest, it's okay to own a lot more stocks if you're in your twenties. Even though stocks have a greater risk, you've got 30 to 40 years to recover any big losses in the market.

A 25-year-old that lost half the value of their investments during 2008 to 2009 had no worries compared to someone who was 65 years old and lost half the value of their investments.

If the 65-year-old was planning on retiring next Friday, if they are invested in 100% stocks and the market tanks on Thursday, they will still probably eat the retirement cake on Friday, but they will be showing up again for work on Monday because they lost a bunch of their retirement savings. Nobody wants that situation.

As you get older, to be healthy and survive longer, you eat a little less meat and potatoes and a little more fruit and vegetables. Salads aren't as exciting as a side of fries, but they are important.

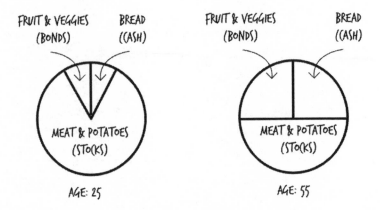

As you get older, to keep from running out of money before you run out of time, you change your asset allocation as you approach retirement from riskier investments, like stock index funds, into more conservative investments, like bond index funds and cash (that don't have as much of a return but also don't carry as much risk).

The bulk of your plate (and your asset allocation) will usually be stocks. While you can choose mutual funds, or index funds, it's using index funds with proper asset allocation that is the sure bet for your future.

Your Portfolio

When you look at your asset allocation, it's across all your money, not just within one type of account. The specific mix of ALL of your investments is called your "portfolio." Imagine you came out of the grocery store with a big grocery cart, a

---

handcart, a flatbed cart, the cart with the two seats for the kids—and they were all loaded with groceries. You take all the groceries from all the carts and throw them in your car. Everything that is in your car—all your groceries—make up your portfolio. It's all the stocks, bonds, and cash you have totaled up, no matter if they are in a 401(k), IRA, bank account, or under your mattress. If you invest in index funds containing stocks, they are considered part of your stock mix.

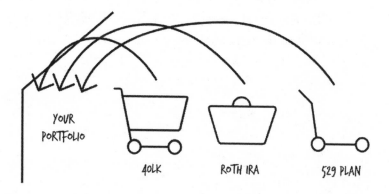

While nobody will ever agree on the perfect portfolio, proper asset allocation is the key factor in building wealth.

Some of the factors that you need to consider before you invest are:

• How much you will invest over time

• How many years until you retire

• How much risk you are willing to take (can you stomach losing 40% of your portfolio?)

- How long you will take to withdraw your money

The more stocks (whether they are in an index fund, mutual fund, or individual company stocks), the more risk. Remember, the more risk, the more reward. The less risky your portfolio, the less money you will make over time.

While there is no correct or perfect asset allocation by age, a general rule of thumb is to subtract your age from 110 and have that amount in stocks (stock index funds, stock mutual funds, and/or individual company stocks). You may find some people say 100 minus your age, and others 120 minus your age.[13] Using 110, your asset allocation would look something like this:

Age	Stocks	Bonds
0-18	100%	0%
20	90%	10%
25	85%	15%
30	80%	20%
35	75%	25%
40	70%	30%
45	65%	35%
50	60%	40%
55	55%	45%
60	50%	50%
65	45%	55%
70	40%	60%
75+	35%	65%

Asset Allocation vs. Diversification

These two terms can be confusing, but since they are two of the most important factors in building wealth, let's look at them side by side to drive the point home.

- You can be *well diversified* with a *poor asset allocation*.

- You can have a *good asset allocation* but be *poorly diversified*.

- You want to have a good asset allocation **and** be well diversified.

Well Diversified + Poor Asset Allocation

You've invested in lots of different stuff (well diversified, lower risk), but if you're young and invested in too many bonds (low return), you'll never make much money.

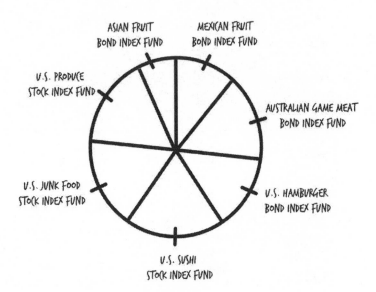

Poorly Diversified + Good Asset Allocation

You've invested in both stock and bonds to minimize big losses while still taking on a tolerable amount of risk, but you haven't spread your money around enough (too many eggs in one basket).

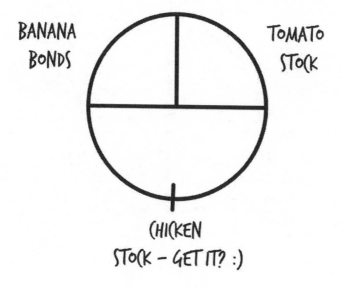

BANANA
BONDS

TOMATO
STOCK

CHICKEN
STOCK - GET IT? :)

Good Diversification + Good Asset Allocation

You've got both stocks and bonds, invested in a lot of different companies, both domestically and internationally. You've got your bases covered.

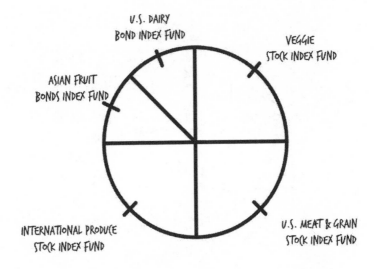

You're now a better cook than the majority of five-star chefs. But some celebrity chefs want to convince you that eating nothing but cake is a great idea. Let's find out why it's not.

25. I'm Young, Why Can't I Just Eat Cake All the Time?

It's true—a 100% stock portfolio will earn more money over a long period of time. The million-dollar question—over what period and for how long? A 100% stock portfolio lost 54% of its value between 2008 and 2009. What if you needed your money during that time? The drag of down years can last for quite some time, but lower-risk investments, like bonds and diversification, can offset that.

A properly diversified mix of stocks and bonds can earn a similar return (slightly lower) to a portfolio of all stocks, but the portfolio with both stocks and bonds is much less volatile—it doesn't have the big gains and losses,[14] which is great if you want to avoid feeling sick, like after Thanksgiving dinner.

An investment portfolio that has an asset allocation of stocks AND bonds is less volatile. When the stock market is down, bonds are usually not. And because bonds are less volatile, your overall portfolio doesn't lose as much value.

BUT—when the stock market is riding high and experiencing huge upswings, if you have part of your investments in bonds and cash, you don't make as much money.

You're best friend or co-worker might be buying a round of drinks for everyone at the bar because *their* portfolio is up 25% this year while *your* portfolio is only up 14%. Or only 11%. **Or not at all!**

Over some shorter periods, especially those of extreme market volatility, the all-stock portfolio has underperformed a blended stock-and-bond portfolio. For example, in the 10 years from January 1, 2000 through December 31, 2009, an investor who was 100% invested in the S&P 500 Index returned a NEGATIVE 1.01% annually. In the same time period, a globally diversified portfolio of stocks and bonds returned 6.08% with a much lower risk.

By investing in more than one group of asset classes—the fancy way of saying invest in both stocks *and* bonds—if one group does poorly, the other group can counteract the losses.

> Does "higher return" mean "better"? IF you were to take 100,000 people and tell them all to not pay for homeowners insurance but to invest in the market an amount equal to their premium, the vast majority of them would come out way ahead. But a few people would be bankrupted by fire, etc. On average, most people would be better off and have more wealth without homeowners insurance. There is higher return by not paying for insurance, but is it better? No, because it's riskier. You don't want to be subject to the risk of having a fire and not being covered even though you know that investing the proceeds on your own is likely to give you more money. The downside of losing your house would be unbearable. Not having homeowners insurance, although it would probably mean more wealth, is not better. For a 40-year-old to be 100% in stocks is not better even though the return is likely to be higher.
> – Barry H. Kaplan, EA, CFP, Chief Investment Officer, Cambridge Wealth Counsel

There are two problems with 100% stock portfolios:

1. You never know when stocks will have a bad run of years. What if you say you're going to go 100% stocks and not touch the investment for 30 years? If in year 21, stocks start a 9-year downward spiral, you would still lose to the blended stock-and-bond portfolio. So you don't make as much money.

2. If stocks do start trending down, you're selling on the way down, losing your money.

Asset allocation is both how you *become* wealthy, and how you *stay* wealthy.

Your Next Step: Remember this: asset allocation is *the* most important investment decision of your life.

Okay, asset allocation is simply picking the proportions of entrees, side items, and desserts you want. In part 5, I'll lay out the proportions to keep you a) from having to decide for yourself and b) well fed for the rest of your life. You've already learned how to make more and keep more than other investors. Let's keep going.

26. Picnics in Winter

You're arranging an outdoor picnic for a family reunion. You decide to hold the event on January 20th in Minnesota because the past two years on January 20th in Minnesota the weather was a balmy 70 degrees (21 degrees C) and sunny. Your family members call you crazy because they know you can't predict with 100% certainty that it's going to be that warm again this year.

But this is how most investors act. They look at what's going on around them, what their neighbor is doing, their co-workers, the person on TV, and try to get in and out of the market based on information about the future that nobody has (except for psychics and tarot card readers). Predicting the ups and downs of the market is like trying to time the weather of a picnic in winter.

If you had $100,000 invested in the stock market in 2008 right before the crash, it was worth $50,000 by May of 2009. As you watched your money disappear day after day, what would you have done?

If you're like most people, you would have freaked out and sold all of your investments to have cash instead. Cash is *safe*. Remember though—cash is *not* safe, as we learned when we discussed inflation. If you never invested again, you would have missed out on watching your money grow to $172,485 as of April, 30, 2016 (the time of this writing).

That's right. Had you done nothing, you're $100,000, which became $50,000, would now be worth $172,485.

We all hate losing money, so what if you could avoid all the **bad days** when it **dropped?** This is what a lot of people do (mistakenly) in order to try to avoid their investments dropping in value. But when the stock market goes down, in the past it has always comes back up. And since nobody knows when the market will come back up, you would miss out on the big gains and the **best days** when it **rises.**

Getting in and out of the market based on what you or someone else thinks is going to happen is called "timing the market." Or "market timing." The opposite of trying to time the market is a "buy-and-hold strategy." You invest (buy), believe in your plan, and stick with it (hold). If the water gets a little rough, you don't jump into the ocean or change directions. You ride through the storm.

Market timing assumes you have information that allows you to predict when the market will go down, so you can avoid losses, or when the market will go up, so you can make money. There are countless studies on how timing the market doesn't work. Most investors buy and sell at the worst possible times.

What if you missed out on the 25 best investing days since 1970 (out of 11,620)? Your average annual return would be half as much.[15] Ouch. Try picking 25 days out of 11,620, and you'll see why it's a fool's errand to hop in and out when you think it's best.

Investing is for long-term wealth building. You buy and buy and buy and buy, until someday you need the money for retirement or some other goal, at which point you sell.

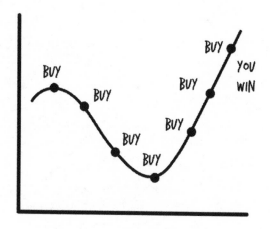

My favorite story of market timing is from a financial advisor whom my mother-in-law-worked for. I subscribed to the firm's newsletter. The financial advisor who "called the 2008 crash" claimed in September 2015 that the DOW would rise to 19,000 points (the market was going to go up). Then *two weeks later* he sent another email to all his clients telling them to sell ALL their stocks and put their investments in cash because he changed his mind and thought the market was going to go down. The old joke is—be wary of someone who has predicted ten of the last three market crashes.

A study of 66,400 investors compared the active traders to the buy-and-hold traders who didn't try to time the market and stayed the course.[16] The most active traders averaged an 11.5% return while passive investors averaged an 18.5% return. Which returns would you like to get?

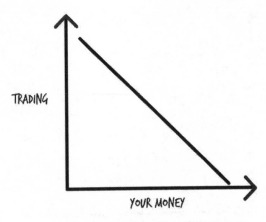

THE MORE YOU TRADE THE LESS YOU MAKE.

When the market shifts, emotions can cloud your decision-making. Bad emotional decisions lead people to buy and sell at the worst times.

Dollar Cost Averaging—The Answer to Timing the Market

If you aren't close to retirement, would you rather the stock market be up right now or down? Most people would say up. And that's why most people lose money at investing.

Let's rephrase the question—*If you want to buy a new TV, would you want to buy it at the full retail price or when it was on sale for 50% off?*

Easy—when it's on sale for 50% off. Because you could buy two TVs, not just one, compared to if you were buying at the full retail price.

When the market is down, you can buy more with the same amount of money.

Dollar cost averaging (DCA) is the simple idea of investing regular amounts of money at regular intervals. If you have money taken out of your paycheck for a retirement plan, you're already doing DCA.

Example: You decide to invest $100 a month in Scott's Donut Shack. The first month, the stock is selling for $20 a share, and you buy five shares. The next month, the stock shoots up to $33 a share, and you buy three more shares. In the third month, the shares go down to $10 a share, and you buy ten shares. The average price you paid per share was $300/18 = $16.67/share.

If the market is down, you can buy more shares of an investment. If the market is up, you can buy less shares. Over a long period of time, we want the shares of our investments to go up in value so that when we sell them, we make big bucks. The more shares we own, the more money we make.

DCA is another method for reducing the risk of investing. The money you invest is spread out over time, no matter what's going on in the market.

Your Next Step: On my website, I have an example showing how DCA worked during the 2008 to 2009 market crash and how it was good for you if you kept on investing during that time. Look at the chart, so you can see dollar cost averaging at work. Go to this URL:

http://scottalanturner.com/what-is-dollar-cost-averaging/

People who invest regular amounts of money at regular intervals end up with more money in the long run than people who try to time the market. You want more money, right? Next find out a way many people have lost it all and how you can avoid the same fate.

27. When Choconuts Goes Bankrupt

If you work for a company and you invest your money in the company stock through the employer retirement plan (401(k)), that's not being smart with your money. You are not diversifying. If the company is Choconut and the company goes bankrupt, your investment is worth $0 in the company.

Companies going bankrupt and their employees losing all of the money they had invested in company stock has happened many times for big companies in recent years. And these were good companies: Enron (2001), Lehman (2008), Worldcom (2002), General Motors (2009). Many employees who had their entire retirement savings in company stock through their 401(k)s lost all of their retirement savings when those companies went bankrupt.

For every story you hear about the grandmother who bought into Microsoft with $10,000 and saw it rise to $2.5 million, or a co-worker's third cousin's barber who bought Apple stock and made $1,000,000, there are thousands of untold stories of real people who lost money (I'm one of them).

If you own individual company stocks or stock in the company you work for—have you read the company's annual report? Are you familiar with the financials of the company, and can you explain them? If the answer is no, how do you know if the company is being run well? And if you don't know if the company is being run well, why would you invest in it?

When you invest in individual stocks, it becomes a part-time job because you're competing against professionals who do it day in and day out.

Your Next Step: If you have individual stocks in your retirement plan, make a note that you need to diversify. You want to avoid a heart attack by investing too much in Choconuts. Ask yourself, "If I own company stock and had an equivalent amount of cash instead of the company stock, would I take the cash and buy company stock?" You got that right—you wouldn't.

Avoid investing in individual stocks. Apple, Facebook, Netflix, Google—yes, they may all seem very tempting. Apple stock was hot in 1983 too—until it lost 75% of its value two years later when Steve Jobs left in 1985. If you think you're pretty smart though and can pick a winner, I've got news for you . . .

28. My Eyes Were Bigger Than My Stomach

Most investors can't help but shoot themselves in the foot.

A yearly report published since 1994 by DALBAR shows consistently that the average investor earns less—in many cases, much less—than the average stock market return.

The average mutual fund investor underperformed the stock market by nearly 5% over the past 20 years. In the year 2014 alone, mutual fund investors underperformed the S&P 500 by a whopping 8.19%![17]

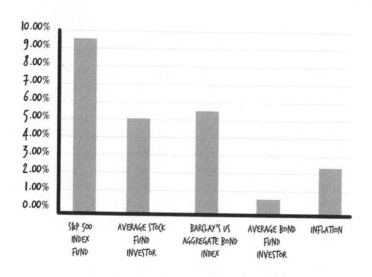

The Cost of Overconfidence

The cost of overconfidence in your own ability can lose you tons of money. How much?

If you had $1,270,000 just ten years ago, overconfidence in trying to pick the best actively managed mutual funds or hot stock **has already cost you $1 million.**

If you had just $100,000 ten years ago, **you've probably cost yourself $78,000.**

When we're talking about the long term, bad investment decisions can cost you *half of your retirement.*

There are a lot of factors that can lead to making poor investment decisions:

- *Herd mentality*—doing what everyone else is doing, even if everyone else doesn't know what they are doing

- *Overconfidence*—believing you can beat the market, even though in chapter 21 I explained the studies showing you can't

- *Impatience*—changing your investment strategy because you didn't see the results you expected to as fast as you would have liked

> If you have decided, believe, and bought into a proven plan
> that works, abandoning the plan after 5 years because it

didn't deliver the expected results doesn't mean the plan is wrong. It's not the plan that is failing, it's you failing to stick with the plan for a long period of time. Wealth is built over decades, not single years.

Your Next Step: If you've been investing, go back from when you first started and see how your returns stack up against the market. Are they better or worse?

If you're starting to realize your investment decisions of the past may be adding up to hundreds, thousands, or even hundreds of thousands of dollars in lost money, I promise to show you the way out. But there are still a few more ways investors lose money that they shouldn't have to. Let's see if those nightly news commercials have gotten to you.

29. Biting Off More Than You Can Chew

Initial public offerings (IPOs) let certain people buy a company's stock before anyone else can (before the general public). It's like the pre-sale of a concert. You join the band's fan club, and you get access to the best concert seats before anyone else when the band goes on tour.

IPOs always make people money, right? False. Katie and I bought into the Vonage (the phone company) IPO. We watched our initial stock purchase of $5,000 become $3,500 in 48 hours. We sold the stock a few days later after losing $1,500.

You may have heard of some of these other types of investments:

- gold
- commodities
- hedge funds
- options trading
- day trading
- penny stocks

Do people make money with these types of investments? Yes. My father-in-law made a lot of money buying and selling gold. He also lost a lot of money.

Do you have to spend a lot of time to make money in these types of investments? Yes. Because you shouldn't invest in what you don't know. And if you decide to hand over your money to a broker or commissioned sales person, remember this—a broker will make you broker. I already shared about the $1,500 I lost in gold and oil commodities.

Day trading, penny stocks—done that too and lost money. I finally got tired of losing money and spending my limited time trying to become an expert in this stuff. That's one of the reasons I became a boring investor. I'm happy *being* the market and not trying to *beat* the market or get rich quick. Or more accurately: get broke quick.

> There are plenty of books on each of these investments. It's not how I invest, it's not what I teach, it's not what I recommend. If you do want to experience the thrill of these types of investments, I would put no more than 10% of your total investments into them (total, not each) as play money.

Unless you plan on becoming a professional investor and make a part-time job out of trying to beat the market (which you know even the Wall Street professionals can't do nearly all the time), decide to skip the fancy stuff. You're now aware of how hard it is. Stick with me, there is one more emotion that gets the best of us. Let's go for a ride on a roller coaster.

30. Getting Gobbled

I'm often on Twitter, sending out 140-character snippets of amazing insight into the world (yeah, right).

Twitter was added to the stock market at the end of 2013. Many times when a new company is added to the stock market, the stock price rises quickly in a short period (unless it is Vonage . . .).

Teresa loves using Twitter and thinks the business is going crazy, so she decides to put all of her money into the stock. She invests $200,000 on November 29, 2013.

By January 3, 2014, her investment has skyrocketed and is worth $320,000. Teresa made $120,000 in a little more than 30 days!

What would you have done in Teresa's situation?

Teresa decides that since the stock has gone up so much, it will continue to go up. Like a gambler in Vegas, she lets her money ride.

But then the stock price starts to go down. By March, Teresa's investment is worth $250,000. Even though she still made $50,000, she lost $70,000 from what she could have had.

Teresa *knows* the stock will go back up, and she can't stand the thought of having just lost $70,000. So she waits.

By May, Teresa's Twitter stock is now worth $150,000. She not only lost the $120,000 she could have made, but she's lost $50,000 of her original hard-earned money. She keeps the stock though because now she needs to make back $50,000 to break even.

By October, she is back up to $250,000. Not wanting to give up and trying to see if she can get back to the $320,000 she had ten months ago, she won't sell.

And so it goes, up and down, up and down. Fast forward to today when Teresa's Twitter stock is now worth $84,000, and she lost money. A difference of $236,000 from the peak.

This story is not uncommon. In fact, the same story has happened to me when I lost $40,000 getting greedy. It doesn't matter if you have $1,000 to invest or $1,000,000, it happens at all saving levels.

Emotion and greed will get the best of you.

If you don't know much about investing or economics, or just don't have time for doing a lot of research, index funds are for you. If you want to become a part-time investor—index funds are *still* for you.

Your Next Step: What do you think? If you made $50,000 owning Twitter stock, would you cash it out or let it ride? It's hard to say when you're not in the situation because it's not real until you're really invested. Ask your friends to see what answers they give.

There are plenty of ways you can sabotage your future. Some might be more intentional, like investing in gold. Some you might not be aware of, like actively managed mutual funds or investments with high fees.

Those things are all on *you*. In the next section you'll discover all the ways *other* people are out to get your money.

PART 4

Managing Your Money Like a Pro: Fad Diets That Leave Your Wallet Weighing Less

31. Try This Hot, New Restaurant—It's Amazing!

Jim Cramer is the host of the nightly stock show *Mad Money* on the CNBC TV network. Jim Cramer is an investing "expert." Yes, he's made a lot of money at picking stocks. Does that mean you should follow the advice of someone just because *they* have made money?

One of my favorite stock segments from Cramer is very entertaining, but the advice is laughable. There is a YouTube video of Cramer responding to a listener question about whether or not the caller should sell his investment in a company called Bear Stearns.[18] The exchange (to paraphrase) goes like this:

Listener: Should I be worried about my investment in Bear Stearns and get my money out of it?

Cramer: NO! NO! NO! Bear Stearns is fine! Do NOT take your money out! . . . Bear Stearns is not in trouble. Don't move your money from Bear, that's being silly.

At the time, Bear Stearns was worth $62 a share. Six days later Bear Stearns was purchased by another company for $2 a share.

If the listener followed Cramer's advice (remember, Cramer is an expert with his own nightly TV show), a $100,000 investment on a Monday would have been worth $3,000 the following Monday. This event happened in 2013.

This gets back to someone trying to *beat* the market. I don't know about you, but if beating the market by picking individual stocks recommended by someone on TV means losing your entire investment, I'll pass.

Hyping stocks is big business. Imagine the cover of money magazines or financial websites without these headlines:

- Two New Stock Picks Just Revealed! (Just Pay Us Money to Find Out What)

- Twenty-eight Best Stocks for Christmas Stocking Stuffers

- Eight Stocks Warren Buffet Is Buying (Or Should Be)

- Two Pet Food Stocks My Cats Are Raving About (And My Dog Too)

Your Next Step: I'm laughing too hard to put a recommendation here. I mean, how else can I convince you not to buy individual stocks? Go watch the video (link is in the reference section).

When you get a hot stock tip, it's already been acted upon. Information is so fast you can bet a stock has gone up or down already by the time you get around to deciding if you should buy or sell. If a professional, like Jim Cramer, could get something so terribly wrong, non-professionals, like you and me, have no chance. There are some people we would like to trust because they may have helped us in the past. But do they have your wallet in mind—or theirs?

32. Rachel Ray's Picture on the Box Doesn't Mean

It's the Best Chicken Stock

I love Rachel Ray—*yumo!*—but a food item at the grocery store with a celebrity chef on the package doesn't mean it has the best ingredients. In fact, you'll find plenty of products with high-fructose corn syrup, tons of salt, and unnatural ingredients in all kinds of pre-packaged celebrity food products. And you'll pay extra for the privilege of buying them compared to the generic store brands.

With investing the line usually goes like this:

"If my fund has a 0.5% higher expense than yours—but I average 12% and you only average 9%—then I win! You lose! End of story! I'm eating steak while you're eating peanut butter sandwiches."

Sigh. Millions of people fall for this BS. If only it were that simple (it isn't). I'll prove it to you right now.

Steve contacted me on Twitter with an investing question. After a few back and forth tweets, I immediately knew what kind of financial services company sold him the investments.

I call these investments, "referred investing professional offerings." RIPOffs, for short.

I asked Steve to tell me what specific mutual funds that RIPOff had sold him, and he sent me a list.

I took Steve's list of investments and used a free service called FeeX (FeeX.com) that analyzes a retirement account or mutual fund and looks for lower-cost alternatives that accomplish the same goal as the mutual fund.

As an example, given a starting investment of $25,000, FeeX found a cheaper alternative to one of the actively managed mutual funds Steve was sold. The less costly investment would have saved Steve $62,000 over a 17-year period.

The choice is yours—do you want an extra $62,000, or do you want to invest in the RIPOff?

There is a natural inclination to believe that because someone helped you with one part of your life, everything they say should be treated as the gospel. The products they recommend must be the best because the person is honest and likes to help others, right?

Like I tell people on my show—don't believe anything any personal finance expert tells you about money until you do your own research.

And that includes believing anything you read in this book.

Trust, but verify.

Your Next Step: You might wait until the end of the book, but check out FeeX.com at some point. It's a free product to check out, and it's pretty neat.

Now that you know you can be overpaying for RIPOffs, now that you know there are cheaper alternatives, make the decision to not get sold on any investment before you thoroughly learn about it and all of the costs. And understand how those costs can add up to hundreds of thousands of dollars you will lose over time. But if you really want to know how badly you're being taken for, let's get loaded.

33. Loaded Baked Potatoes

What if you walked into a pizza place to pick up a nice, hot pizza, and the guy at the counter took a slice out of the box and ate it in front of you?

Sadly this situation occurs every single day to unknowing investors.[19]

Many mutual funds have HUGE upfront commissions ("sales load") that go into the pockets of salespeople. Often the ones pushed by celebrity-endorsed services or big name brand investment companies charge you 4.0% to 8.5% for the privilege of buying a product that can't beat the market over time. Many mutual funds (not index funds) are a huge rip-off with their high fees. Mutual funds with huge up-front commissions are an even bigger rip-off because you can find plenty of no-load ("commission-free") equivalent funds.

High costs don't mean high quality.

If you walk in the front door with $100,000 and buy these kinds of mutual funds, the value of your investment when you walk out the door is $94,500. Remember compounding? You're money has to work that much longer and harder first to get back to $100,000 before you can start making money.

Mutual funds with the big up-front commissions are called "A-Shares." Sometimes you can tell them apart because they have the **letter A** at the end of the name. Tough, huh?

The first time I taught people about A-shares on my show, I received a flurry of angry emails from listeners. They looked at their investments and realized they were paying these huge up-front commissions and didn't even know it. One person moved his wife's old 401(k) to a new investment advisor and then got hit with a 5.25% commission. In his own words:

I'm not happy.

I feel stupid.

Please share this message, so others do not make the mistake.

Example: You have $100,000 to invest from an old 401(k) after you left your job. A nice salesperson sells you a mutual fund with a 5.25% up-front load (sales commission). The salesperson keeps $5,250 to pay for their vacation. The starting value of your investment is now $94,750. How long did you have to work to earn that $5,250 you just paid anyway?

Brokers may tell you a mutual fund with a load performs better because it has a smart fund manager. The commission goes to the salesperson, not the fund manager, and there is no relationship between the two.

> You don't have to pay a 5% commission for an inferior product that won't make you as much money as an index

fund. Most actively managed mutual funds can't overcome the handicap of the sales commissions and high fees that eat away their returns each year. Active Anne rarely looks better than Passive Paula, and Passive Paula is going to be healthier and wealthier over time.

Okay, what about that argument that paying a commission is fair because it's how the person is paid for their services?

My response—I'm showing you how to get better advice that costs less, for better products that cost less and will make you more money over the long term. You win, they lose.

Your Next Step: If you have some investments, check if you are paying for A-Shares or not.

There is a quick way to determine the difference between a salesman and a trusted advisor. In chapter 42, you'll know immediately if someone has your best interest in mind. A person can have a good heart and teach you about investing, and still direct you to inferior products. And often they are able to convince you their products are better with the promise of great returns. Let's see why that's a big myth.

34. Voted Best-Tasting Burger Since 1934!

Chasing returns and trying to beat the market is an expensive business. Expensive for *you*. Trillions of investing dollars are at stake, and billions are spent on advertising and slick, glossy brochures to capture your money. Actively managed mutual funds are run by people who try to beat the market (get a better-than-10% return). Remember in chapter 21 I explained it isn't possible over time to beat the market, but it doesn't keep active managers from trying?

You can't argue facts.

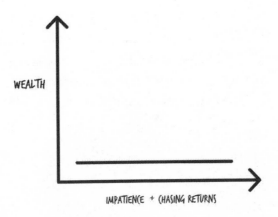

In the fifteen years prior to 2011, forty-six percent of actively managed funds shut down because of lousy performance.[20]

Additionally those funds that show 12% returns don't take into account fees, trading costs, taxes, and other expenses you pay. The *real* return is much less.[21]

Can you make 12% or more in good growth stock mutual funds? The answer will surprise you. Watch my video series **The 10% Reality, the 12% Reality, and the 13% Reality (The Good, the Bad, and the Ugly)** to find out.

www.scottalanturner.com/eastwood

I'll repeat what you might hear or read:

Don't let anyone tell you that you can't get a 12% rate of return or that it's impossible in good growth stock mutual funds.

I will show you exactly where to find a mutual fund with a 12% rate of return. I will also show you where the person selling it to you is taking a 5.25% commission. If all you were to pay attention to was the 12% rate of return and the expense ratio, you would still be having the wool pulled over your eyes. The people endorsing those funds receive huge compensation for doing so.

When you invest in passively managed index funds, using dollar cost averaging, you are not trying to chase 12% returns or the next hot stock tip. You've bought into the academic research of a proven strategy over time. Good past performance of actively managed funds is a matter of luck.

Past performance does not guarantee future returns.

While there are no guarantees when it comes to investing, the research is pretty clear that an actively managed mutual fund cannot beat the market over time (so they can't beat passively managed index funds). Yet when most people invest, they look at the average annual return of a mutual fund as the most important consideration choice as to whether an investment is a good choice or not.

If someone asks you if you want to be an average investor and get average returns, the answer to quote from the only chick flick I like (*Pride and Prejudice*):

YES!!! A thousand times—YES!!!

I hope I've drilled that point home that being average and getting the average returns of the stock market (being the market) is proven in study after study to beat the people who claim they can *beat the market.*

It doesn't make you foolish if you go for the average—it makes you a smart investor.

It's human nature to be wowed by marketing and numbers that look good on paper. But when you do the math and start digging in, 1+1 = 0. Since you're reading this book, you're becoming financially literate and won't be left with a stomachache. What other ways do you pay more than you should for investments? Let's find out.

35. Premium Grocery Store Shelf Space

When you visit a grocery store or drugstore, you will see some chips and products placed in prominent places—sometimes right in the middle of the aisle. You can't help but see them. Companies pay extra money for this prime shelf space in an effort to sell more products. But because they have to pay more for the prime potato chip locations, those costs get passed along to you in the form of higher-priced chips.

If someone tries to sell you on a particular investment—the Chocolate Mutual Fund instead of the Vanilla Mutual Fund—you need to ask them, "Why this fund?"

A salesperson's first loyalty is to their firm—their employer. If they don't make the company money, they lose their job. A salesperson's next duty is to themselves. If they don't make themselves money, they can't pay their bills. A salesperson's last duty is to you—you're last on the list.

The following quote is from a 2005 press release from California Attorney General Bill Lockyer, who was suing American Funds for not telling investors the truth about broker payments. The lawsuit claimed American Funds paid brokers $426 million to push their mutual funds:

> "American Funds dressed up these arrangements with
> fancy names like 'execution revenue,' 'target commissions'

> *or 'Broker Partnership Payments,' " said Lockyer. "But*
> *when you look beneath the cloak of legitimacy, the*
> *payments are little more than kickbacks to buy preferential*
> *treatment. Investors deserve to know that. The law*
> *American Funds violated is based on that simple*
> *principle."[22]*

Choose investments from people and companies that put your money over their interests. An investment provider, financial planner, or broker can't be objective when they have to choose between selling you on something to able to pay their mortgage or not.

Your Next Step: Ask yourself, "Why pay a broker a hefty commission when I can purchase the same thing myself online for pennies?"

Okay, you've got the Kevlar vest, football helmet, umbrella, light saber—you're protected from the "experts" trying to confuse you, the ones more interested in their own retirements than yours. If you've had some hiccups in your investing journey, that's okay. Let your mistakes drive you to grow your money and build a solid investing plan going forward. Let's get to the reason you started reading to begin with—"Whe

PART 5

How to Beat Wall Street:

A Recipe for Success

36. Store-Bought or Homemade?

Let's get down to it—*Where do I put my money? What do I put my money in?*

The more options you learn about, the more confused you will become. I'm skipping the intermediate and advanced stuff. I'll show you how to dissect your 401(k)/403(b), 457, and what to do if you don't have a company retirement plan.

It's going to be like choosing between frozen pizza, a delivered pizza, or making your own dough.

I'll give you a couple of options for the "set it and forget it" crowd, i.e., those of you that want an easy solution that you can get going with in 10 to 20 minutes. Yes, you got that right: 10 to 20 minutes. These options are "robo-advisors" and "target date funds."

If you want a little more control and/or you want to be a little more involved (not much, but a little), I'll give you the simple process for making solid investment choices.

But before you decide *what*, you have to first decide *for how long*.

37. How Long to Age Cheese and Wine

When I visited my good friend Jordan in Switzerland, one of the places on our weeklong vacation was the city of Gruyere. Gruyere is the home of Gruyere cheese. With cheese, the length of time it ages in the big cheese warehouse is the only difference between mild and sharper flavors. The longer cheese is aged naturally, the sharper and more pronounced the flavor becomes. Some cheeses are aged for a few weeks, and some might age for as long as a year. Time is the only variable, just as it is with a good wine or dry-aged steak.

Part of deciding *how* to invest is first deciding *how long* you will invest—good investments, like excellent cheese and wine—need to be aged. So, how much time do you have? If you are age 20 and want to retire at age 40, you will make different choices than someone that is age 50 and retiring at 65.

Your "investment horizon" is how long you plan on holding your investments before you start needing the money for something. The longer your horizon, the greater risk you can take early on to have a higher reward later. A long-term horizon allows you to recover from bad years in the economy. If you need your money sooner and your horizon is shorter, it's better to choose lower risk investments to avoid losing money when you'll need it.

What choices will be different? Your asset allocation. When you're young, you'll have a little more meat and potatoes (stocks). As you approach retirement, you'll want to have more side items on your plate (bonds) and salad (cash).

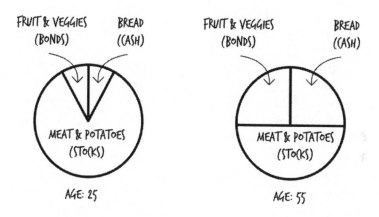

A general guideline, which I already introduced to you in chapter 24, is to subtract your age from 110, and that's the amount of stocks you should own.

If you are age 35, then 110 − 35 = 75, so 75% of your money goes into stocks, and 25% goes into bonds and cash.

If you are age 70, 110 − 70 = 40, so 40% of your money into stocks, and 60% goes into bonds and cash.

Remember, if you're age 70, you might live another 10 to 30 years! To keep inflation and taxes from eating up your savings, you have to make sure your money continues to grow, so you don't run out of it. And when you hit retirement, you will never sell all your investments and keep everything in cash. The best course of action will be investing until you pass away.

> This guideline is just that, a guideline. Investment money is money put away for five years or more. For any money you need to save for the short term—to buy a car, a house down payment, a vacation—the money should never be invested in the stock market. If you have a $40,000 house down payment in the stock market and you are about to buy a home, what happens if the stock market drops 25% over the next week? You now have $30,000 for a down payment, and you will continue to be known as a renter.

Your Next Step: Have you thought about when you want to retire? Ask a parent, sibling, partner, or good friend when they plan on retiring and how they plan on getting there. You're probably going to hear a lot of "I'll probably have to work until I die." That should fuel your fire to change your life today, so you have the option of working if you *want* to, not because you *have* to.

Once you've picked a retirement date, it's time to start investing. Let's make the simplest investing decision of them all.

38. Frozen Pizza

Target date funds are like frozen pizza. You take what's in the box, heat up the oven, and cook it. It's the easiest way to eat. You may find one in your 401(k) plan, or you can sign up for one on your own.

When you sign up for a target date fund, you pick the year you want to retire, the "target": 2020, 2025, 2030, 2035, 2040, 2045, 2050, 2055. The year you pick determines the asset allocation of your investment money, between stock, bonds, and cash equivalents.

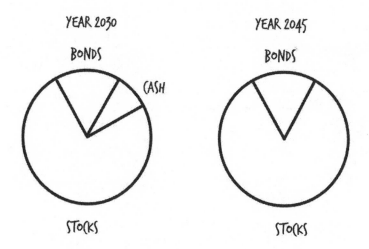

With these investments, as you approach retirement, the investment firm automatically shifts your investments to be more conservative (less stocks, more bonds).

Why? If the market tanks the day before you retire, you don't want to have to say to your boss, "Oops, I think I'd like to work for a few more years." A target retirement fund avoids that scenario.

The great thing is the asset allocation is done for you automatically. The simple steps are:

1. Create your account.

2. Set up automatic investments to make deposits every month.

3. Wait for retirement.

You can find a lot of information on target date funds. Many financial advisors will give you reasons why they don't like them. Fair enough. But if you don't use a financial advisor, don't want to pay a financial advisor, and you want to set-it-and-forget-it, a target date fund is the perfect place to get started investing. You can set one up in ten minutes.

What's inside a Target Date Fund?

A target date fund is a "fund of funds." For example, a target date fund that I would use is the Vanguard Target Retirement XXXX Fund. The XXXX is the date you want to retire, for example, 2045. In the Vanguard fund, you will find four other funds. Your asset allocation (the percentage of your money

---

invested stock funds, bond funds, and cash) depends on the date you want to retire.

- Vanguard Total Stock Market Index Fund Investor Shares: **54.0%**
- Vanguard Total International Stock Index Fund Investor Shares: **36.0%**
- Vanguard Total Bond Market II Index Fund Investor Shares: **7.0%**
- Vanguard Total International Bond Index Fund Investor Share: **3.0%**

Total—100.0%

Okay, scary stuff. Not really because you already became an expert in asset allocation and diversification earlier. You know you need to be diversified to reduce your risk—eating at all the buffets via index funds. And you need good asset allocation—having a balanced meal plan of stocks and bonds.

If you plan on retiring in 30 years, you would be invested in 90% stocks and 10% bonds. In stocks, you're 54% US stocks and 36% international. In bonds, you're 7% US bonds and 3% international. Easy stuff.

Every company has its own formula for deciding how much stocks and bonds. Fidelity's 2045 fund would have you in 94% stocks and 6% bonds.

If you are just getting started, it's more important to get started than worry about the particular asset allocations in various target date funds. The more important thing to look at is the fees.

Why You Should Use a Target Date Fund

- It helps you avoid most of the mistakes investors make.

- It's easy.

- It doesn't require you to pay someone for advice.

Why You Shouldn't Use a Target Date Fund

- Some have very high fees (especially in 403(b) plans). Fair enough—there are a lot of target date funds with high fees, especially the ones found in company retirement plans.

- If you have investments in multiple places, like a 401(k), Roth IRA, and an individual brokerage account, your asset allocation and/or diversification could be incorrect. For example:

  o In your 401(k), you put 100% of your investments in a target date fund

  o And in your Roth, you put 100% of your investments in a US index fund

  o And in your brokerage account, you have a mix of domestic and international investments.

- It can make you an uneducated investor, and uneducated investors lose money. The content in this book will help you figure out what's going on in a target date fund. As long as you understand the funds ingredients—fees, asset allocation, and funds within the funds—you're a smart investor.

The people who say all target date funds are bad are often interested in selling you something else. As usual, follow the money to see why the advice is being given. There are some great target date funds with very low fees.

Your Next Step: If you have a target date fund in your retirement plan, see what yearly fees are being charged. Are they high (greater than 0.50%)? Or low (below 0.50%)? Check back to chapter 23 on how high fees steal your wealth over time.

Target date funds are great because they keep you from making a lot of the mistakes resulting from bad asset allocation. If you want an alternative to a target date fund that gives you a little more variety, read on.

39. Pizza Delivery

I mentioned earlier that on the Star Trek Enterprise there is a food replicator to create meals for you. Great as that is, the replicator doesn't prevent you from ordering hot-fudge sundaes and cookies for every single meal.

In the past few years, a new type of service has sprung up called the "robo-advisor." Online services have sprung up from both new start-up companies and from old investment firms looking to keep up with the times that allow you to put in your age, goals, and risk tolerance. The computer will invest your money based on these variables. Over time, as with a target date fund, the service automatically adjusts your investments. Robo-advisors can give you a few more options over a target date fund, like adding extra pepperoni to your pizza.

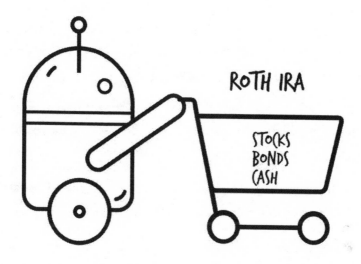

A robo-advisor is a good option if you are setting up a Roth IRA, IRA, or a plain old investment account.

One of the appeals of a robo-advisor is the low fees and low minimums required to get started investing. Many bigger firms have minimums of $1,000 or more, which locks out a lot of people trying to get started investing without much money. Robo-advisors are perfect for the new and seasoned investor.

I like Betterment because it takes ten minutes to set up an account, and I like the interface. What I like best though is Betterment invests in Vanguard funds. They kind of act like a middleman, so you pay a little more in fees. But it's still cheaper than a lot of other options, and it costs nothing to get started.

You'll find people hate robo-advisors too, just like people can hate target date funds. It's unimportant for this discussion. This book is the let's-get-a-meal-cooked-and-on-the-table-and-start-eating-so-we-can-have-a-rich-meal-and-a-rich-life book. It's not the 1,152-page *Joy of Cooking* with every recipe you could ever want with every type of ingredient known to humankind.

There is nothing wrong with getting started investing with a robo-advisor. For someone who can't afford or doesn't want a financial planner guiding them, a robo-advisor gets the job done.

But, like target date funds, robo-advisors are geared towards people who don't want to know a lot about investing.

What they offer is a one-size-fits-all approach—you get what they serve you. As your wealth increases (which it will if you learn anything from this book), it's time to consider a personal chef.

If you choose to go with a robo-advisor, you can open an account with Betterment at www.betterment.com or by calling 888.428.9482. It will take you 10 to 15 minutes to get up and running. There are other robo-advisors as well (Wealthfront is another good one). I always tell people to do their own research and pick the solution that works best for them.

Robo-advisors are the future today. But some people want more choice as to what they invest in. Now it's time to take a look at how you can have greater control over your investments by selecting your own ingredients.

40. Rolling Your Own Dough

If you would prefer to have more control over selecting your investments, instead of using a target date fund or robo-advisor, this two-step process will get you there.

This option is good if you are setting up a Roth IRA, IRA, or plain old investment account.

Step 1. Pick an investing company—where to buy groceries.

Just as you have a variety of restaurants to dine at, there are a lot of choices in the investing world about where to put your dollars to work for you.

Fidelity and Vanguard have the lowest fees you can find. They are in a constant battle to see who can offer the lowest fees—good for you and me as the consumers because it saves us money. I'm going to use these two companies as examples.

Full-service companies, like Morgan Stanley, Merrill Lynch, and Goldman Sachs, are the equivalent of shopping at Whole Foods (or Whole Paycheck, as it's known by some) and hiring a private chef to make your meals. You get more personalized service, but it costs you a ton more money.

You can open an account with Vanguard at www.vanguard.com or by calling 877.662.7447.

You can open an account with Fidelity at www.fidelity.com or by calling 800.343.3548.

Both places handle different types of accounts—IRAs, Roth IRAs, and individual accounts. Make sure you pick the right account to set up (explained in chapter 44).

Step 2. Picking your investments—what to put in your shopping cart.

Entree, side items, dessert—that's a meal. Let me tell you about a low-cost, well-rounded meal plan called the "three-fund portfolio."

The three-fund portfolio is something that will beat most other investors. It is simple, has basic asset classes, and is very popular because of its tax efficiency and low fees.

You invest in three funds:

- total stock market index

- total bond market index

- total international stock market index

With these three funds, you're buying a little bit of everything. Talk about diversification! Every buffet, every entree, every side item, every dessert—everything.

How much of each?

If you ask different people to choose a three-fund portfolio, you will get different answers as to which funds and how much of each.

These choices and allocations are based on maximizing returns while minimizing risk. Remember, asset allocation is the most important investment decision you will make.

These are guidelines. You are unique. Your timeframe is unique. Your risk tolerance is unique. Your personal finance situation is unique. But these are great options to get you going, overcoming the fear of investing, and giving you bang for your buck. You can't engineer the perfect portfolio because nobody can predict what the market will do tomorrow, let alone ten years from now.

A young investor's asset allocation 80/20 (80% stocks/ 20% bonds)

- 64% total stock market
- 16% total international stock market
- 20% total bond market

A middle-aged investor 60/40 (60% stocks/ 40% bonds)

- 40% total bond market
- 12% total international stock market
- 48% total stock market

An investor in early retirement 40/60 (40% stocks/ 60% bonds)

- 60% total bond market
- 8% total international stock market
- 32% total stock market

An investor in late retirement 20/80 (20% stocks/ 80% bonds)

- 80% total bond market

- 14% total stock market
- 6% total international market

You've got the proportions of what to buy. Now let's pick the specifics of what investments to choose.

If you go with Vanguard, these are the names of the funds you would invest in:

Vanguard

- Vanguard Total Stock Market Index Fund (VTSMX)
- Vanguard Total International Stock Index Fund (VGTSX)
- Vanguard Total Bond Market Fund (VBMFX)

And if you prefer Fidelity, you would pick the following:

Fidelity

- Fidelity Spartan Total Market Index Fund (FSTMX)
- Fidelity Spartan Global ex US Index Fund (FSGUX)
- Fidelity Spartan US Bond Index Fund (FBIDX)

A list of three-fund portfolios using index funds from other fund companies is included in the resources section.[23]

Note: *Be aware of any minimum investment required by each fund. The investor shares of most Vanguard funds require a minimum investment of $3,000.00. Lower-cost Vanguard Admiral shares typically require a minimum of $10,000.00. If you will have difficulty meeting these minimums, you may want to consider an all-in-one single-fund portfolio (target date fund) until you accumulate enough so that this is not an issue.*

That's pretty much it. It's no different than going to the grocery store and buying fish, tater tots, and a bag of salad. You can do it yourself online or call one of the companies and have someone help you set up your account. You've now created:

- a portfolio with good returns at lower risk and volatility

- a well-diversified portfolio—you own a little of everything

- a good asset allocation—you've balanced risk and reward

- a portfolio with very low yearly expenses

- a portfolio that will beat actively managed fund(s) over time

- a portfolio you can automatically invest in, so you can spend your time on more important things

- a simple portfolio

According to Meir Statman, Santa Clara (California) University finance professor who studies investor behavior, in regards to the three-fund portfolio:

> *You can make it really simple, be well-diversified, and do better than two-thirds of investors. For many, that is a sense of relief. Other people think of it as throwing in the towel. There is a competitive streak in them that says, "I can do better than that," and being in the top one-third is not going to get you any medals and is not going to make you rich.*[24]

A three-fund portfolio doesn't take any special expertise to build. It's simple, boring, and if you invest often over time and stick with it, you will build wealth.

Is this the best investment solution ever? Is it the best investment solution for you? I address that very question at the end of this section. But first, if you still can't decide what to do . . .

41. Pizza, Pizza, or Pizza?

By now you should be through the confusion of investing. You may still be wondering, "Okay, what should I do? Just tell me!"

This table is a quick comparison of the three different choices I presented. The great thing for you is—**they are all great choices.**

If you remember the principles of a healthy, balanced diet—

- good asset allocation

- passively managed index funds with low fees

- good diversification

—all three choices give you those ingredients. They are what you need to build wealth and keep more of your money.

If you just want someone to pick one for you, then go with the Vanguard Target Date Retirement Fund. If you can't make the minimum investment, go with Betterment.

Features	Target Date Funds	Robo-advisors	3-Fund Portfolio
Low fees	Varies	Yes	Yes
Passive index funds	Varies	Yes	Yes
Automatic rebalancing	Yes	Yes	No
Automatic investing	Yes	Yes	Yes
Advisor assistance	No	Varies	No
Set it and forget it	Yes	Yes	No
Available for employer retirement plan	Yes	No	No
Available for IRA/Roth IRA	Yes	Yes	Yes
Available for college savings plans	Yes	No	Varies
Available for taxable brokerage account	Yes	Yes	Yes

What if you want a little extra hand-holding? How do you know if a person with the heart of a teacher really has your best interest at heart? More than likely, they believe they are sincerely helping you, but they don't know nearly as much about investing as you do now. Let's quickly learn how to know . . .

42. Gordon Ramsay, Chef-Boyardee, or You?

Oprah has a personal chef that whips up anything she wants to eat, any time of day. Man, that would be nice. A personal chef gets you out of having to cook for yourself, but it would be pricey.

There are different types of chefs that are available to help you in the kitchen. We already talked about robo-advisors, the robots that are pre-programmed to make a couple of meals based on your preferences. But they don't take requests. You eat what they serve.

Up a notch (or down, depending on your perspective) is you. You can be in charge of the meal planning, grocery shopping, and cooking. Everything you've read up until now makes you a smarter chef than 99% of the population.

Next we have a broad class of people who fall under the category of "financial advisors." Anybody can call themselves a financial advisor. My cat is a financial advisor. So is the tree in my front yard. And the guy who picks up my garbage.

Beware of any professional touting their accomplishments as being one of America's "best" or "top" financial planners or advisors. One investment advisor submitted an application on behalf of his dog to the Consumer's Research Council of America to be named one of "America's Top Financial Planners." The dog—Max Tailwager—received the award.[25]

MY CAT RIKER IS READY TO ADVISE YOU

Financial advisors have no obligation to do what is in your best interest. Advisors have to meet what's called a "suitability standard." Some of the names they go by include:

- Investment advisors

- Investment/retail brokers

- Fee-based Certified Financial Planners

- Investing professionals

- Supreme overlords

Despite what they may call themselves:

- they get paid by selling you more stuff;

- they may be limited to selling only products approved by their company;

- they may not be selling you what's in your best interest; and

- they may sell you higher-priced products when lower-cost options exist.

As you would expect, this group always has the same argument to convince you they are the best at managing your money:

"I'll gladly pay someone 4% a year if they can make me 16% a year on my investment."

So would I, if it were possible and proven over time—which it isn't based on all the studies referenced so far.

The biggest problem with most advisors is they have a conflict of interest. They *have* to sell you investments in order to pay for *their* mortgage, *their* car payment, *their* yacht, *their* retirement, *their* kid's college tuition . . .

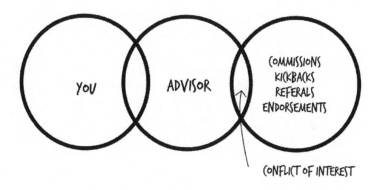

How do you find someone that doesn't have a conflict of interest and will put your money, your retirement, your wealth as the *single* and *only* focus of their advice? Simple—ask them if they are a fiduciary.

The Fiduciary Standard—Food Safety Laws

Up the food chain at the highest level are people who follow the fiduciary standard. This group is legally bound to do what is in your best interest. It's the highest code of conduct. If you want to know if someone is putting your interest first, ask them if they follow the fiduciary standard and get it in writing. If they don't, leave.

Also, you have advisors that are provided by some of the investment companies. For example, if you called Vanguard and said, "Hey, help me get started," you would be able to talk with someone who will walk you through the process and make suggestions. They won't help you decide what to pick in your company 401(k) though.

Someone following the suitability requirement is making sure the investment is suitable for the client. But that doesn't prevent brokers from selling their own or inferior products when lower-cost alternatives exist. Guess what? Lower-cost alternatives almost always exist. It's like putting a soda company in charge of regulating soda in schools. Does the soda company want to sell more or less of their products in schools? More, of course. They want to make money. Screw kids' health.

You work too hard for your money to trust someone in a suit with a nice smile or someone endorsed by a celebrity.

You only have to follow the money to see who doesn't like the new Department of Labor rulings requiring 401(k) administrators to be held to a fiduciary standard: big banks, big commission-based Wall Street firms (not the discount brokers), and RIPOffs—those that make the most money by having things stay just the way they are. It's good for you and bad for them.

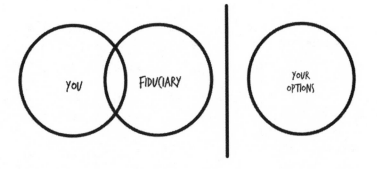

Katie and I have worked with a fee-only Certified Financial Planner since 2005. **Fee-based** CFPs are different than **fee-only** CFPs. Fee-only CFPs don't make commissions or try to sell you on something that they get a kickback from or compensation for. Fee-only CFPs charge you a fee for their services, and they must follow the fiduciary standard. They are who I tell my show listeners to work with. I don't get paid referral fees or make any commissions, money, advertising, or endorsements from the CFP organization. Fee-**only** is the **only** one I recommend you work with. Makes it easy to remember.

Your Next Step: If you currently have an advisor or broker, ask them if they are a fiduciary. And if you ever look for an advisor, make sure they are a fiduciary.

If and when you decide an advisor is right for you, you should be wary of anyone that doesn't steer you towards low-cost index funds, such as those found at Vanguard and Fidelity, most Exchange Traded Funds (ETFs), or Dimensional Fund Advisor (DFA) funds.

Buy, Rent, or Sharecropping

Great fiduciary advisors will help you stop acting like a kid in a candy store and grabbing every investment that looks tasty.

STICKING TO YOUR PLAN

A study by Vanguard found that investors who had an advisor earned 3% more annually than DIYers.[26]

But that advice comes at a cost.

The fees can vary

- Sharecropping—percent of investments they manage (1% per year, as an example) *"Sharecropping" is a system of agriculture in which a landowner allows a tenant to use the land in return for a share of the crops produced on the portion of land.*

- Rent—monthly charge ($79, for example)

- Buy—flat fee consultations ($125+)

Fee-only CFPs that act as fiduciaries can be found on several websites:

- XYPlanning Network.com

- Garrett Planning Network

- NAPFA

Note: Going to someone else can be helpful, primarily because that person isn't you. They can refresh your memory of why you started down a particular path to begin with. They can suggest a course correction. They can point out the things you can't see. It's much easier to recognize the mistakes other people are making than recognizing the mistakes you might be making.

Good, personalized advice comes with a cost. But what if you just want some guidance in the right direction or someone to look over your shoulder occasionally? There is a reason you might want that, and I'll share it with you.

43. Attending Cooking Classes

I pay to go to the doctor every year and have him tell me if I need to cut back on the cookies and Ben & Jerry's ice cream. Thankfully he hasn't told me I need to yet.

You will someday want some personalized advice. I call this "Do It Yourself Plus" (DIY+) because if you've read this far and you get on the path to building wealth, you will want some expert third party checking on your investment choices. You can't get that information from *any* book or *any* robo-advisor. Everyone needs a coach or an advisor to help them get to the next level. Even professional athletes at the top of their games, like Olympic medalist swimmer Michael Phelps, still have coaches.

When? If I had $10,000 or more, I'd gladly pay a fee-only CFP for an hour of their time to look over my plan and offer some advice. That's just a made-up dollar amount not based on any study. If you own a car, you would pay to have the oil changed and a yearly service. You pay to have your teeth cleaned two times per year. You pay for yearly health physicals. If you bought a home, you would pay $400 for a house inspection.

Good financial advice isn't a cost, it's another type of investment.

In chapter 42, I mentioned the study by Vanguard showing people who used an advisor had 3% better returns than people who didn't. The biggest reason is because a good advisor helps you stick to your plan. A good advisor keeps you from making poor, emotional decisions when the market is tanking. A good advisor will prevent you from selling all your investments and putting your money in your best friend's new cupcake shop. A good advisor does just that—provides good advice. And that advice can be worth much more than what it costs you for the advice.

My advice—find a good advisor, at least for a periodic review of your plan.

I'll make up a number, but if an advisor charges $150 an hour and I have to pay them $300 to review my asset allocation and the funds I've selected based on my investing goals, that's a bargain. You can lose $1,000 in an instant if you invest $20,000 with a RIPOff.

The sooner in life you learn this stuff, the more money you'll have when you retire. Some advisors add value by putting together more advanced portfolios (beyond the scope of this book).

Your Next Step: Make a note to yourself to get a checkup at some point in the future. It doesn't have to be today, next month, or this year. But someday getting a quick review of your investment choices can be valuable to your wealth. Put it on the calendar.

Congratulations—you've come a long way! The vast majority of investors don't know what you now do. Now let's figure out the strategy of how to divide up your money into different investing carts.

44. Shopping at ALDI

ALDI is a grocery chain known for having a very limited selection of products. If you go to Walmart, you might have your choice of twenty types of peanut butter, but at ALDI you'll get to pick from one. Your employer's retirement plan usually has a limited selection as well.

What you will pay in taxes in the future is a topic of great debate. Unfortunately, nobody knows. The tax rates have changed 6 times in the past 20 years. Sometimes up, sometimes down. It's a safe conclusion taxes will go up or down in the future.

The people who will be paying the most (not as a percent of their income, but as a $$$$ amount) are the people who have the most money. That's going to be you because you'll be following this proven plan to build wealth. If your goal is to get $1,000,000 in investing, you're probably going to pay a lot of taxes when you start withdrawing your money that hasn't been taxed yet.

By investing in tax-free retirement investments, like a Roth IRA or Roth 401(k), you don't have to worry about what the government is going do with tax rates over the next several decades.

By investing money that isn't taxed (401(k)) *and* money that has been taxed already (Roth IRA), you cover your bases. In retirement you'll have some flexibility when you start pulling money out of those accounts to keep your taxes lower.

Think of it this way: you have a deep freezer at your home. Any time chicken is on sale, you buy a lot of it and store it in the freezer. Then beef goes on sale, and you stock up on it. A couple years from now, if beef is expensive, you thaw out the beef you already own and eat it. You continue to buy chicken from the store because the prices are low, so you leave your frozen chicken untouched. If chicken prices go up and beef goes down, you do the opposite—buy beef from the store and eat your frozen chicken.

By having a frozen storage supply (investments) of both beef (taxable investments, like a 401(k)) and chicken (untaxed investments, like a Roth IRA), you can minimize your grocery bill (your taxes) at any time.

> A full discussion of tax planning and minimizing taxes in your investments is beyond the scope of this book.

How do you know if your 401(k) sucks? You can find out by using BrightScope.com. BrightScope provides an independent retirement plan rating comparing your plan to others.

What if you have an existing employer retirement plan like a 401(k)? Most financial advisors will give you this advice when you're building up to your 15% to 20% savings rate:

1. Max out your employer retirement plan UP UNTIL THE MATCH. If there is no company match or you don't have an employer retirement plan, skip to the next step.

If the match is 6%, contribute up until the point you are saving 6% of your paycheck.

    a. If you're married and you both have company matches, same thing—up until the match for both of you.

2. Max out a Roth IRA.

Take money from your take-home pay and fully fund a Roth IRA. If you are married fully fund one for each of you.

The current limits are $5,500 a year per individual. If you're 50 or older, you can kick in an extra $1,000 as a *catch-up* provision.

Stop—here's why. If there is a company match, it's free money—get it!

But you're employer plan is paid with pre-tax money. It reduces your taxes now and you pay taxes on it in retirement as you withdraw it. A Roth IRA is paid with money you've already paid the taxes on. The Roth grows tax-free and when you take the money out to spend it, there are no taxes to pay. You beat the taxman! The Roth is the best thing going, other than free money from your employer.

3. Go back and max out your 401(k).

4. If you have even more money, put it into a taxable account (plain old investing account) at one of the discount brokers. That means you're just using one of the different types of carts to hold your money. There are no tax advantages though.

Your Next Step: After you get any employer match, open a Roth IRA. If you can meet the minimums required by the low-cost brokerages (Vanguard and Fidelity), sign up with them. Or you might go with a robo-advisor like Betterment. Either way, it takes ten minutes to set up.

That was pretty easy—just directing different amounts of your money to different investment carts as your income grows. Let's dig into your employer retirement plan to see if we can optimize your investments.

45. Lunch at the Office Cafeteria

Everyone's situation is unique, but that doesn't mean there aren't some easy options for you. Many people get stressed out about 401(k)s because sometimes there are dozens of choices to pick from, and it is your future. Your boss isn't going to sit down with you and walk you through what you should do. And if they offer, politely decline because the advice they give (unless they also read this book) may not be for your best financial future.

Generally you should pick a target date fund, unless:

1. There isn't one to pick.

2. You just love the idea of picking your own investments.

3. It has high fees.

If you're new to investing or you don't have a lot of time or interest in picking your own funds, picking just a single target date fund is your best option. Simply select the one fund with your target retirement date, and you're done. The limitation of the target date funds is that they are one-size-fits-all. If you want to be more or less aggressive, a target date fund is not right for you. But it's better than nothing.

Automated 401(k) Management

If you prefer a service that will manage your portfolio for you, I suggest you check out www.blooom.com.

For a low monthly fee, Bloom will analyze your 401(k) and select the best investment options for you based on the funds available, your risk tolerance, and your retirement date.

What I would suggest if you choose to use the service is to try it for a month. Have it update your 401(k), check the recommendations, and then decide if you want to keep the service.

Professional 401(k) Management

Hiring a fee-only CFP to review your 401(k) options is another choice. It will be the most expensive, but the expert opinion of a human can have a huge impact on the growth of your 401(k) investments.

At the end of the day, you have to ask yourself, "Do I want to spend my time on this? If not, how much am I willing to pay someone to help me figure it out?"

Picking Your Own 401(k) Funds

If you're willing to take on more risk or you want to take on less risk, you'll need to select individual funds and handle your own diversification and asset allocation.

1. Pick your asset allocation. If you're 30, you'll invest more heavily in stock mutual funds than bond mutual funds compared to a 55-year-old.

2. Determine how you will diversify—what percent in domestic, international, and bonds.

3. Don't buy company stock (discussed in chapter 27).

4. Choose index funds when you can.

5. If you don't have index funds available, review your mutual fund options. You can ignore the short-term (1-,3-, or 5-year) returns listed in the funds. The important number is the long-term return because past performance is not an indicator of future gains. A hot fund can be hot one year and cold the next. What happens over time should be your focus. Aim for picking funds that have low fees with good track records over a 10-year period.

Your Next Step: *Now* that you *know* how to properly pick good low-cost funds in your employer retirement plan and how to do proper asset allocation, see what adjustments you might need and make them. When in doubt, try out Blooom.com or seek out a fee-only CFP for assistance.

Once your investment carts are off and running, it's time to make sure they stay on course. Turn the page and discover how you can keep things running smoothly in just one Sunday afternoon a year.

46. Are You Getting Enough Veggies?

Once a year, it's time to review your eating plan based on your current weight. Based on the review, you might decide to eat a salad instead of a burger once a week. Or you might feel you can get away with another pint of ice cream now and then.

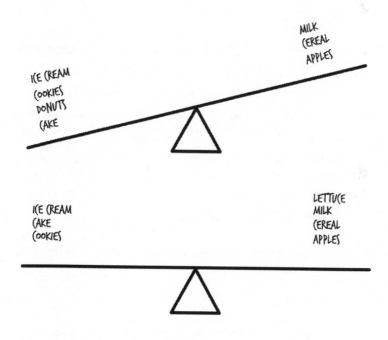

We call this "rebalancing." Over time your portfolio (like your body) may become out of balance. Your asset allocation will change due to how the market behaves (it's normal). Since nothing is more important than how you allocate your assets in your portfolio, you need to occasionally make adjustments to get it back to where you want it to be (your goal weight).

Rebalancing is bringing your portfolio back to your desired asset allocation.

Personally I hate eating vegetables, but I force myself to do it. Thankfully rebalancing is much easier than choking down more broccoli.

Here's an example:

Your desired asset allocation is 70% stocks and 30% bonds. The market is having a great year, and your stock funds go up. At the end of the year, instead of a 70/30 split, you have an 80/20 split (80% stocks, 20% bonds). You haven't changed your investing plan, but your investments did change. You can correct this in a couple ways:

1. Invest more money and buy what is necessary to get back to your goal asset allocation.

2. Sell one or more investments and use the money from the sale to buy what is necessary to get you back to your goal asset allocation.

A couple in their early forties has an asset allocation goal of 75% stocks and 25% bonds in their investment portfolio. At the end of 2015, their portfolio was 85% stocks and 15% bonds. Their stock value grew. GOOD! However, their new asset allocation, 85% stocks and 15% bonds, no longer aligns with their goals. The couple increased risk exposure in stocks. The fix—sell 10% of the stocks and buy bonds. The result will bring the couple back to their asset allocation goal, 75% stocks and 25% bonds.

Your Next Step: Check your asset allocation each January. Based on your financial goals, determine if rebalancing is necessary. If the allocation has only changed 2% to 3%, I don't make any changes. My personal preference.

Note: If you are invested in a target date fund or invested at a robo-advisor, rebalancing is done automatically for you.

Rebalancing should take you 90 minutes or less, once a year.

What should you do the other 364 days of the year? Forget about checking your investments. You are now a long-term investor with a superior strategy. Be confident in your plan, and avoid the emotional roller coaster by not checking your balances. If they are up, you will be happy. If they are down, you will question your decisions. If you don't look, you'll be just fine and will avoid making irrational decisions.

Your Next Step: If you have some investments already, check to see if you need to rebalance them.

Wow! You've figured out the not-so-secrets to becoming a rock-star investor. You're in the band! In the next few pages, I'll share with you a few more things, so you can have this locked down. First, one dollar at a time.

47. Good Cooking Takes Time

You can buy pre-cooked BBQ ribs from places like Costco that taste—*meh* . . . Or you can wake up at 3 am and start smoking ribs yourself to have a delicious lunch ready by noon. If you want amazing ribs, you either have to stand in line at a restaurant that started cooking them at 3 am, or you have to do it yourself. The best ribs take time to cook, but they are worth the wait.

As an investor, you will no doubt have some expectations of what you would like to happen. Allow me to set some realistic expectations for you, so you're not disappointed by the results.

You won't make money quickly.

"Where is the profit you made from Betterment?" That's an exact question someone asked me after I had been investing with Betterment for 12 months.

My response—*I don't know, and I don't care.* I believe in the system as I explained it:

- Proper asset allocation

- Investing early and investing often (dollar cost averaging)

- Not trying to time the market

- Staying the course

- Investing in passively managed index funds

Based on research and what I have learned from over a decade of passive investing, I know that with the investment strategy I follow, used by millions of others, over a period of decades I will come out ahead of any other investing strategy.

I don't know or care what my investments do day to day, week to week, month to month, or even year to year. I do know that over a long period I will beat actively managed investors all the time. What my profit is from last year is of no importance. I'm not cashing out my investments tomorrow, or in ten years even. I believe in the plan, so I follow the plan. If I had a bad year, I'm not selling, and if I had a good year, I'm not selling. So why does it matter? It doesn't.

But you will make money slowly.

Go back to the compound interest examples in chapter 5. Look at the very small rate by which money appears to grow in the first few years and the tremendous rate by which it grows in later years.

For example, after 10 years, a $500 per month investment (not much more than the average car payment) has become $99,934. But what about by year 20? It's $359,136. And if you wait 30 years, you'll have $1,031,439.

Is there a better way to bake a cake?

What's the best way to bake a cake? Ask a dozen bakers, and you'll get a dozen different answers.

You will find some people that agree with the strategies in this book, and some that disagree. One thing is certain—you will get conflicting advice on what you should do with your money. Everyone's way is best—just ask them.

Here's an easy test to see if the person that is giving you advice may have a conflict of interest—follow the money.

- Are they making a commission if they sell you a certain product?

- Are they getting paid by recommending one product over another?

- Are they getting paid advertising fees or kickbacks?

- Are they pressuring you to make a sale?

Brokers make you broker. And brokers go by many titles (see chapter 42) other than "broker." Most people are interested in their own money at the cost of yours. Don't let a fancy title fool you.

You are the best advisor for your money.

Automation, compounding, sticking with your plan—you have the tools and knowledge to do this. But you may be left scratching your head and wondering, "Why haven't I heard this before?" What you need to do then—find out where this information has been hiding.

48. Is This a Secret Recipe?

As I stated earlier, there isn't any new information in this book that hasn't been around for decades. You may ask yourself why you've never heard it before. I'll walk you through the reasons.

#1. Lack of education

Nobody teaches this stuff in school. You won't learn it from your employer.

Your boss is probably just as in the dark as you were, or they might think they are a really great investor, so they try to beat the market. You now know that isn't possible.

#2. Money

If Coke or KFC gave out their top-secret recipes for their products, what would happen to their businesses? They would lose money.

There are hundreds of millions of dollars at stake every year selling products, advice, and services. Keeping you in the dark helps keep money in someone else's pocket (not yours). Convincing you higher-priced, inferior products are better than low-cost index funds are how many so-called advisors pay for their mortgages and retirement. The people with the biggest yachts in the harbors near Wall Street belong to the brokers, traders, and salespeople—not the customers.[27]

#3. It's not sexy, it's boring

Active investing is exciting, like trying a deep-fried margarita or fried butter at the Texas State Fair (the Texas State Fair is known for the yearly competition of best new fried food). Passive investing is like plain vanilla ice cream. It's plain and kind of boring compared to a deep-fried banana split.

Active investing makes the nightly news and sells more magazines and books. All passive investing does is make more *money*. But because it's simple and easy, there's not much to discuss about it on a daily, weekly, or monthly basis.

I'll take more money, what about you?

I don't believe you, so-and-so said this:

I'm always skeptical of new ideas too. I genuinely hope you **don't** believe me because I want you to do your own research and fact check what I've said. I've included a bibliography at the back of this book citing my sources in order to prove that everything I've told you is accurate to the best of my knowledge. I challenge you to prove me wrong.

Here's a final tidbit—I use math to help me make decisions. I am so convinced of the investing philosophy in this book, it's exactly how I invest. Using my little investment calculator on my website, I figured out that **if I thought I could get a 12% return on my investments**, I would end up with an **additional $20 million** decades from now.

I'll repeat—because of compound interest, that dream of beating the market, or the 12% people claim you can get, would be worth an additional **$20 million** to me.

Would I be willing to risk $20 million if I thought active mutual fund managers and people claiming you can get a 12% return were right? Not no, but *heck no*. I'd want that money. And I would buy myself a Gulfstream Jet. But I don't believe the hype, and neither should you. I guess I'm stuck flying coach with American Airlines.

Never quit.

Always doubt.

Trust but verify.

You'll be glad you did.

If you still have doubts—good! I hope that means you'll do some more digging on your own. Let's take a look at some people who do use this investing strategy.

49. The Great Chefs of the World

You wouldn't think I would make all these promises about simply building wealth without some proof right? The proof is in the pudding—as they say.

Aside from millions of individual investors that follow the simple strategies in this book, there are quite a few big wigs that follow this investing strategy:

Corporate

- AT&T Inc.
- Boeing Corporation
- Citigroup
- Exchange Bank
- Iberdrola USA
- Kellogg Company
- Merck
- MLC
- National Telecommunications Cooperative Association
- PepsiCo, Inc.
- PPG Industries, Inc.
- Sandia Corporation
- TIAA-CREF
- TimkenSteel Corporation
- Tribune Company
- Verizon Communications, Inc.
- WellPoint, Inc.
- Yum! Brands, Inc.

Nonprofits

- Baptist Foundation Alabama
- California Wellness Foundation
- Carnegie Mellon University
- Chicago Community Foundation
- Creighton University
- Gonzaga University
- Idaho Community Foundation
- Kansas Health Foundation
- Lucile Packard Foundation for Children's Health
- Misericordia Home Endowment
- New Haven Community Foundation
- Public Policy Institute of California
- San Francisco Foundation
- Simon Fraser University
- Surdna Foundation
- Toledo Community Foundation
- United Way of Palm Beach County
- University of Miami
- University of Pittsburgh Medical Center
- Wallace Foundation
- Western Michigan University Foundation

Public

- Alaska Permanent Fund Corporation
- Arizona State Retirement System
- City and County of Kalamazoo
- City and County of San Francisco
- City of Baton Rouge
- City of San Diego
- City of Seattle
- Florida State Board of Administration
- Illinois Municipal Retirement Fund
- Los Angeles Department of Water & Power System
- Marin County Employees' Retirement Association
- Maryland State Retirement Agency
- Mississippi Public Employees Retirement System
- Montana Board of Investments
- Municipal Fire & Police Retirement System of Iowa

- Nebraska Investment Council
- North Dakota State Investment Board
- Nova Scotia Association of Health Organizations
- Oregon Office of the State Treasurer
- South Dakota Investment Council
- St. Paul Teachers' Retirement Fund Association
- Teachers' Retirement Allowances Fund
- Utah State Retirement Systems

Pension Plans (Taft-Hartley)

- Bakery & Confectionary Union and Industry International Pension Fund
- California Public Employees Retirement System (CalPERS)
- Florida State Board of Administration
- IBEW Pacific Coast Pension Fund
- Illinois State Pension Fund
- Indiana State Council of Plasterers and Cement Masons Pension Fund
- Laborers' District Council & Contractors' Pension Fund of Ohio
- Local Union #226
- Maine Public Employees Retirement System
- Montgomery County Employees Retirement Plan in Pennsylvania
- National Electrical Benefit Fund
- National Retirement Fund
- New York State Common Retirement Fund
- North Carolina Retirement System
- Southern Nevada Culinary & Bartenders Pension Fund
- Union Electrical Industry Master Trust

So you can see you're in good company. However, you may be wondering, "Is that it? Is that all I need?" For most people, yes, that's it. For a small percentage, you might want to take things a little farther. That's for you to decide after reading the next chapter.

50. Advanced Cooking Techniques

The simplest way to be healthy is to eat right and exercise. Would you agree with that?

At its basic level, diet and exercise contribute to better health. But what about this statement: "Eating blueberries instead of pineapple as an afternoon snack will result in lower insulin levels and reduced cortisol levels, causing a lower fat production"?

I have no idea if that statement is scientifically correct. I put a bunch of health terms I'm familiar with together, and it sounds pretty impressive.

The point is this—blueberries and pineapple are both fruit. Fruit is supposed to be good for you. But is some fruit better for you than others? And if so, what fruit, how much should you eat, and at what time of day?

This book gives you the principles necessary for establishing a foundation of investing, and successful investing, at that. And while it's superior to most of what's out there, you can expand on this foundation to help compound your money even more. What I can't do is teach basic math, trigonometry, algebra, calculus, and differential equations in one book. No worries—what comes after the basics boils down to other ways to allocate your assets with different types of index funds. But it would cause the book to get into the equivalent of braised duck recipes and making baked Alaska. There is a time and place for those, but not in this book.

Staying out of overwhelm is an important part of your taking action. Get started eating right and exercising. Do your blueberry vs. pineapple research later.

Will you have the perfect portfolio if you follow the guidelines I provide in this book?

Not no, but heck no.

The perfect portfolio, the perfect financial plan, is the one that is perfectly tailored to your unique goals and needs, and can only be achieved by you. Preferably you work with someone that doesn't have an emotional connection to your money as you do. The information you've discovered in this book will protect you from the wolves trying to slaughter your retirement.

You will be hard-pressed to **not** build wealth if all you did was read this book and follow the guidelines. But is that it? I challenge every listener of my show to continuously discover more about money, and I issue the same challenge to you.

- If you have a large amount of money/a large portfolio, you can benefit from including some other index funds in your asset allocation.

- If you are a high-income earner, you can benefit from tax-exempt bonds.

- If you are approaching retirement, you can benefit from inflation-protected investments (TIPS).

- You can also benefit from REITs (real estate investment trusts).

But those things for right now are barriers to getting started. Get started! All of those types of investments are available as index funds at the discount brokers.

You are unique, your timeframe is unique, your risk tolerance is unique, and your personal finance situation is unique. Bake the cake. You can add the fancy frosting flowers later by learning how to make fancy frosting flowers from reading cookbooks and watching Food Network, or from working with a fee-only CFP to show you how they would make fancy frosting flowers for your cake. It doesn't take that much more time, and it's not that much harder. If you want to keep going, let's find out where to go next.

51. Cooking at Home Once in a While

The people who have your back have no interest in taking your money through investment products and services. If you take a little time to check the research of leading finance professors and academics, you'll find it jives with the content in this book. University professors' only desire is to look like rock stars in the eyes of their peers—other people in the academic community. So they can't toss out poorly researched information, or they will be ridiculed, like a skinny kid with acne (like I looked back in high school).

The more you know about money, the less likely you are to be ripped off and the more likely you are to get more money and grow your investments. You will be in control.

Remember—you can hear information that sounds sincere, but it can be sincerely wrong.

Commit to reading 60 minutes a *month* about investing. While I would love it if everyone would watch one hour less TV each week and read an investing book, I feel anyone can stomach one hour a month. That's 12 hours a year, out of 8,760 hours each year. Not much. Those 12 hours will make you 100 times smarter than every other person on the planet when it comes to investing.

What should you read?

This book gave you the foundation you'll need to understand any of these more advanced books. Here are some of my recommendations, in order of preference:

- *The Millionaire Next Door* by Thomas J. Stanley—this is the most important book you'll ever read. It has nothing to do with investing practices, but it will change your outlook on money.

- *The Smartest Investment Book You'll Ever Read* by Daniel R. Solin

- *The Bogleheads' Guide to Investing* by Mel Lindauer, Michael LeBoeuf, and Taylor Larimore

- *Random Walk Down Wall Street* by Burton Malkiel

- *Wise Investing Made Simple* by Larry E. Swedroe

- *Uninvested: How Wall Street Hijacks Your Money and How to Fight Back* by Bobby Monks

Your Next Step: Head to Amazon or your local bookstores and buy one of those books, or check it out for free at your local library.

You're probably now the smartest investor in your office, in your neighborhood, and in your family. Congrats on a job well done! To wrap up with one final cooking metaphor, so you can get on with implementing your newfound knowledge, let's put the icing on the cake.

52. The Icing on the Cake

The icing on the cake is—you can build wealth.

There may be times when you are tempted by the slick advertising, compelling salesperson, or market downturn to abandon your investing plan. Have faith in math, research, and Spock logic (from *Star Trek*). Emotion is a wealth killer. The benefits of long-term investing using a passive strategy, proper asset allocation, and low-cost index funds have been proven without a doubt. If you start to have doubts, double back and see if the original plan was flawed or if you're having a temporary emotional breakdown. For most investors, the get-out, bail-out, cash-out, trade-out mentality is what hurts them in the long run—not the occasional big market dip.

Knowledge without action might give you a grocery list, but unless you go shopping and make the meal, you'll go hungry.

You can now take control of your investments with very little time and effort, but whatever you do, make sure you do something. Take action to become your own investment professional. Doing or saving a little each day or month is enough to get started on the path to achieving financial freedom.

I would love to hear from you and answer any questions you may have! My contact information is available at **GoAskScott.com**

ROCK ON!

Scott Alan Turner

Free Dessert

Don't miss out on the great, free extras you can get right now:

How to Save $1,000 in One Week—My simple guide on how you can save money on your everyday expenses. Join thousands of other people and start saving today!

11 Habits of Millionaires—What have millionaires done differently than other people to achieve their wealth? The answers may surprise you.

Step-By-Step Investing Checklist—A short summary of the steps outlined in this book so you can make sure you're on track with your investing goals and don't miss anything.

The Lost Chapter!—One of the important topics about investing that didn't make the cut because it was a little too much (*boring*).

BONUS ONLINE CONTENT: Download the bonus content at scottalanturner.com/99

Appendix A: Master of Cookies

Taste me you will see—

More is all you need.

—"Master of Puppets" by Metallica

I really do love desserts, so I'm including my favorite cookie recipe. And I wanted to write the only investing book ever that includes a baking recipe because I'm weird like that. Bon appétit.

*Makes 20–24 **MASSIVE** cookies.*

Ingredients

- 3 1/2 cups all-purpose flour
- 1 teaspoon baking soda
- 1 teaspoon cinnamon
- 30 tablespoons unsalted butter, at room temperature (3.75 sticks or 15 oz.)
- 2 teaspoons salt
- 1 1/2 cups packed dark brown sugar
- 1 cup granulated white sugar
- 4 teaspoons vanilla extract
- 2 large eggs, plus 2 large egg yolks
- 16 ounces of baker's semi-sweet chocolate (1 lb. or two 8-oz. boxes)
- 2 cups pecans

Instructions

1. Heat oven to 375 degrees F.

2. When the oven is heated, toast the whole pecans 5 to 8 minutes. Be careful not to overcook; they will burn easily. Heat them just enough to bring out the flavor (you can tell by the smell). After the pecans have cooled, chop them up into chunks. *Chunks = about 4 to 8 pieces per pecan.*

3. Chop the chocolate bars into chunks.

4. Sift or whisk flour, baking soda, salt, and cinnamon together in a large bowl.

5. Beat the butter and sugars in a mixer with the paddle attachment on low for 2 minutes, then on medium-high for 4 minutes until the mixture starts to get fluffy.

6. Add the vanilla to the mixer and beat for 30 seconds. Scrape down the sides of the bowl.

7. Add the eggs and egg yolks, one at a time, to the mixer, beating for 30 seconds each. Scrape down the sides of the bowl after adding each one. You don't need to separate the yolks/whites.

8. With the mixer on low, add the dry ingredients until incorporated.

9. Remove the bowl from the mixer. Add in the chocolate chunks and pecans, hand-mixing until evenly distributed.

10. The cookies can be baked on cookie sheets or baking sheets lined with parchment paper.

11. Take 1/4 cup of batter and make mounds, placing each mound 4 inches apart on the sheets. The batter should be in a mound (like a mound of mashed potatoes), not a ball.

12. Bake in the oven until the edges start to brown, 10 to 14 minutes. The center will be a little soft, the edges a little crispy. Remove from the oven and let the sheet cool 3 to 5 minutes, then transfer to a wire rack. Serve warm or at room temperature.

Appendix B: The Word on Index Funds

American Association of Individual Investors: "It should come as no surprise that behavioral finance research makes a strong case for buying and holding low-cost, broadly diversified index funds."

Mark Balasa, CPA, CFP: "That three-pronged approach is going to beat the vast majority of the individual stock and bond portfolios that most people have at brokerage firms. There is a certain elegance in the simplicity of it."

Christine Benz, Morningstar director of personal finance: "By buying total-market index funds—one for US stocks, one for foreign stocks, and one for bonds—investors can gain exposure to a huge swath of securities in three highly economical packages."

Bill Bernstein, author of *The Four Pillars of Investing:* "Does this [three-fund] portfolio seem overly simplistic, even amateurish? Get over it. Over the next few decades, the overwhelming majority of all professional investors will not be able to beat it."

Jack Bogle, Vanguard founder: "The beauty of owning the market is that you eliminate individual stock risk, you eliminate market sector risk, and you eliminate manager risk. . . . There may be better investment strategies than owning just three broad-based index funds but the number of strategies that are worse is infinite."

Warren Buffett, famed investor: "I'd rather be certain of a good return than hopeful of a great one. . . . Most investors are better off putting their money in low-cost index funds. . . . There seems to be some perverse human characteristic that likes to make easy things difficult."

Scott Burns, financial columnist: *"The odds are really, really poor that any of us will do better than a low-cost broad index fund."*

Jonathan Burton, *MarketWatch*: "There are plenty of ways to complicate investing, and plenty of people who stand to make money from you as a result. So just think of a three-fund strategy as something you won't have to think about too much."

Andrew Clarke, co-author of *Wealth of Experience:* "If your stock portfolio looks very different from the broad stock market, you're assuming additional risk that may, or may not, pay off."

Jonathan Clements, *The Wall Street Journal* columnist and author: "Using broad-based index funds to match the market is, I believe, brilliant in its simplicity."

John Cochrane, American Finance Association president: "The market in aggregate always gets the allocation of capital right."

Consumer Reports Money Book: "Simply buy the market as a whole."

Phil DeMuth, author of *The Affluent Investor:* "Buying and holding a few broad market index funds is perhaps the most important move ordinary investors can make to supercharge their portfolios."

Laura Dugu, ambassador and co-author of *The Bogleheads' Guide to Retirement Planning:* "With only these three funds in your investment portfolio you can benefit from low costs and broad diversification and still have a portfolio that is easy to manage."

Charles Ellis, author of *Winning the Loser's Game:* "The stock market is clearly too efficient for most of us to do better."

Eugene Fama, **Nobel Laureate:** "Whether you decide to tilt toward value depends on whether you are willing to bear the associated risk. . . . The market portfolio is always efficient. . . . For most people, the market portfolio is the most sensible decision."

Paul Farrell, author of *The Lazy Person's Guide to Investing:* "Where does [**Nobel Laureate**] Fama invest his retirement money? 'In index funds. Mostly the Wilshire 5000.'"

Rick Ferri, *Forbes* columnist and author of six investment books: "The older I get, the more I believe the three-fund portfolio is an excellent choice for most people. It's simple, cheap, easy to maintain, and has no tracking error that would cause emotional abandonment to the strategy."

Benjamin Graham and Jason Zweig, authors of *The Intelligent Investor:* "The single best choice for a lifelong holding is a total stock-market index fund."

Alan Greenspan, former Federal Reserve chairman: "Prices in the marketplace are by definition the right price."

Mark Hebner, author of *Index Funds:* "A diversified portfolio which captures the right blend of market indexes reaps the benefit of carrying the systematic risk of the entire market while minimizing exposure to the unsystematic and concentrated risk associated with individual stocks and bonds, countries, industries, or sectors."

Hulbert Financial Digest: "Buying and holding a broad-market index fund remains the best course of action for most investors."

Sheldon Jacobs, author of *No-Load Fund Investing:* "The best index fund for almost everyone is the Total Stock Market Index Fund. . . . The fund can only go wrong if the market goes down and never comes back again, which is not going to happen."

Kiplinger's Retirement Report: "You'll beat most investors with just three funds that cover the vast majority of global stock and bond markets: Vanguard Total Stock Market, Vanguard Total International Stock Index, and Vanguard Total Bond Market Index."

Lawrence Kudlow, CNBC: "I like the concept of the Wilshire 5000, which essentially gives you a piece of the rock of all actively traded companies."

Professor Burton Malkiel, author of *Random Walk Down Wall Street:* "I recommend a total-maket index fund—one that follows the entire US stock market. And I recommend the same approach for the US bond market and international stocks."

Harry Markowitz, **Nobel Laureate:** "A foolish attempt to beat the market and get rich quickly will make one's broker rich and oneself much less so."

Bill Miller, famed fund manager: "With the market beating 91% of surviving managers since the beginning of 1982, it looks pretty efficient to me."

E.F. Moody, author of *No-Nonsense Finance:* "I am increasingly convinced that the best investment advice for both individual and institutional equity investors is to buy a low-cost broad-based index fund that holds all the stocks comprising the market portfolio."

The Motley Fool: "Invest your long-term moolah in index mutual funds that are designed to track the performance of a broad market index."

John Norstad, academic: "For total-market investors, the three disciplines of history, arithmetic, and reason all say that they will succeed in the end."

Suze Orman, author and financial advisor: "One of my favorite index funds, Vanguard Total Stock Market (VTSAX), has a total expense ratio of 0.06%."

Anna Pryor, *The Wall Street Journal* journalist: "A simple portfolio of three funds. It may sound counter-intuitive, but for the average individual investor, less is actually more."

Jane Bryant Quinn, syndicated columnist and author of *Making the Most of Your Money:* "The dependable great investment returns come from index funds which invest in the stock market as a whole."

Pat Regnier, former Morningstar analyst: "We should just forget about choosing fund managers and settle for index funds to mimic the market."

Ron Ross, author of *The Unbeatable Market:* "Giving up the futile pursuit of beating the market is the surest way to increase your investment efficiency and enhance your financial peace of mind."

Paul Samuelson, **Nobel Laureate:** "The most efficient way to diversify a stock portfolio is with a low-fee index fund. Statistically, a broadly based stock index fund will outperform most actively managed equity portfolios."

Gus Sauter, former Vanguard chief investment officer: "I think a very good way to gain exposure to the stock market is through the Total Stock Market Portfolio on the domestic side."

Bill Schultheis, author of *The Coffee House Investor:* The simplest approach to diversifying your stock market investments is to invest in one index fund that represents the entire stock market."

Charles Schwab, businessman, investor, and founder of Charles Schwab Corporation: "Only about one out of every four equity funds outperforms the stock market. That's why I'm a firm believer in the power of indexing."

Chandan Sengupta, author of *The Only Proven Road to Investment Success:* "Use a low-cost, broad-based index fund to passively invest in a little bit of a large number of stocks."

Professor Jeremy Siegel, author of *Stocks for the Long Run:* "For most of us, trying to beat the market leads to disastrous results."

Dan Solin, author of *The Smartest Portfolio You'll Ever Own:* "You can get as simple or as complicated as you'd like. You can keep it very simple by owning just three mutual funds that invest in domestic stocks, foreign stocks, and bonds. That's precisely what I recommend in my model portfolios."

William Spitz, author of *Get Rich Slowly:* "Few are able to beat a simple strategy of buying and holding the securities that comprise the market."

Professor Meir Statman, author of *What Investors Really Want:* "It makes sense to have those three funds. What makes it hard is that it seems too simple to actually be a winner."

Robert Stovall, investment manager: "It's just not true that you can't beat the market. Every year about one-third do it. Of course, each year it is a different group."

Larry Swedroe, author of seventeen financial books: "Over the last 75 years, investors who simply invested passively in the total US stock market would have doubled their investment approximately every seven years."

Peter D. Teresa, Morningstar senior analyst: "My recommendation: A fund that indexes the entire market, such as Vanguard Total Stock Market Index."

Wilshire Research: "The market portfolio offers the best ratio of return to risk."

John Woerth, Vanguard director of public relations: "We would agree that this three-fund approach offers most investors a prudent, well-balanced, diversified portfolio at a low cost."

Jason Zweig, *The Wall Street Journal* journalist and author of *Your Money and Your Brain:* "I think a total stock market index fund is not only the simplest, but the very best core investment for most people."

References

[1] "Poll: 28% of Americans Have Not Read a Book in the Past Year," *The Huffington Post,* October 7, 2013, accessed May 17, 2016, http://www.huffingtonpost.com/2013/10/07/american-read-book-poll_n_4045937.html.

[2] "Personal Saving Rate," Economic Research Federal Reserve Bank of St. Louis, last modified April 29, 2016, accessed May 25, 2016, https://research.stlouisfed.org/fred2/series/PSAVERT.

[3] Ashleigh Schmitz, "The National Pizza Index: What's the Average Price of an American Pie?" Parade, March 27, 2014, accessed May 25, 2016, http://parade.com/274999/ashleighschmitz/the-national-pizza-index-whats-the-average-price-of-an-american-pie/.

[4] Historical Performance of the S&P 500 2007–2009 Monthly Returns," Yahoo Finance, accessed June 26, 2016, http://finance.yahoo.com/q/hp?s=%5EGSPC&a=00&b=3&c=2007&d=05&e=24&f=2010&g=m

[5] J.B. Maverick, "What Is the Average Annual Return for the S&P 500?" April 24, 2015, accessed May 31, 2016, http://www.investopedia.com/ask/answers/042415/what-average-annual-return-sp-500.asp.

[6] Marc Davis, "How September 11 Affected the US Stock Market," Investopedia, last modified September 2, 2011, accessed May 25, 2016,

http://www.investopedia.com/financial-edge/0911/how-september-11-affected-the-u.s.-stock-market.aspx.

[7] Eugene F. Fama and Kenneth R. French, "Luck Versus Skill in the Cross Section of Mutual Fund Returns," Journal of Finance 65, no. 5 (October 2010): 1915–47.

[8] Christopher B. Philips, Francis M. Kinniry Jr., David J. Walker, Todd Schlanger, and Joshua M. Hirt, "The Case for Index-fund Investing," Vanguard, March 2015, accessed May 26, 2016, https://personal.vanguard.com/pdf/s296.pdf.

[9] Javier Espinoza and Simon Constable, "Mutual Funds' Five-Star Curse," The Wall Street Journal, last modified September 7, 2014, accessed May 25, 2015, http://www.wsj.com/articles/how-funds-with-5-star-morningstar-ratings-10-years-ago-have-fared-1410120116.

[10] Laurent Barras, Olivier Scaillet, and Russ Wermers, "False Discoveries in Mutual Fund Performance: Measuring Luck in Estimated Alphas," The Journal of Finance 65, no. 1 (2010).

[11] Ty A. Bernicke, "The Real Cost of Owning a Mutual Fund," Forbes, April 4, 2011, accessed May 26, 2016, http://www.forbes.com/2011/04/04/real-cost-mutual-fund-taxes-fees-retirement-bernicke.html.

[12] "Vanguard 500 Index Fund Admiral Shares," Vanguard, accessed May 26, 2016, https://personal.vanguard.com/us/funds/snapshot?FundId=0540&FundIntExt=INT.

[13] Robert Laura, "Time to Return to Old School Asset Allocation: 100 Minus Your Age," Forbes, September 22, 2015, accessed May 26, 2016, http://www.forbes.com/sites/robertlaura/2015/09/22/time-to-return-to-old-school-asset-allocation-100-minus-your-age/#bbcbfec1547f.

[14] "Harry Markowitz," Wikipedia, last modified May 22, 2016, accessed May 25, 2016, https://en.wikipedia.org/wiki/Harry_Markowitz.

[15] Michael Batnik, "How Missing Out on 25 Days in the Stock Market over 45 Years Costs You Dearly," MarketWatch, last modified February 17, 2016, accessed May 25, 2016, http://www.marketwatch.com/story/how-missing-out-on-25-days-in-the-stock-market-over-45-years-costs-you-dearly-2016-01-25.

[16] Brad M. Barber and Terrance Odean, "The Behavior of Individual Investors," September 7, 2011, available at http://ssrn.com/abstract=1872211 or http://dx.doi.org/10.2139/ssrn.1872211.

[17] Stephanie Ptak, "2014 Dalbar Quantitative Analysis of Investor Behavior," Dalbar, April 9, 2014, accessed May 26, 2016, http://www.dalbar.com/Portals/dalbar/cache/News/Press Releases/2014QAIBHighlightsPR.pdf.

[18] "Mad Money Host Jim Cramer: Don't Be Silly on Bear Stearns!" YouTube, March 28, 2013, accessed May 26, 2016, https://www.youtube.com/watch?v=V9EbPxTm5_s&nore direct=1.

[19] Bobby Monks, Uninvested: How Wall Street Hijacks Your Money and How to Fight Back (New York: Penguin, 2015), 86.

[20] "The Mutual Fund Graveyard: An Analysis of Dead Funds," Vanguard, January 2013, accessed May 26, 2016, https://personal.vanguard.com/pdf/s362.pdf.

[21] "The 10% Reality, the 12% Reality, and the 13% Reality (The Good, the Bad, and the Ugly)", Scott Alan Turner, July 2016, http://www.scottalanturner.com/the-12-percent-reality

22 "Attorney General Lockyer Sues American Funds for Not Telling Investors Truth about Broker Payments," State of California Department of Justice Office of the Attorney General, last modified March 23, 2005, accessed May 25, 2016, https://oag.ca.gov/news/press-releases/attorney-general-lockyer-sues-american-funds-not-telling-investors-truth-about.

23 "Three-fund portfolio," Wikipedia, last modified April 18, 2016, accessed May 26, 2016, https://www.bogleheads.org/wiki/Three-fund_portfolio.

24 Jonathon Burton, "Three Mutual Funds that End the Guesswork," MarketWatch, December 5, 20016, accessed May 26, 2016, http://www.marketwatch.com/story/story/print?guid=F0 47C5E4-3F49-451A-9A69-FD8FBF2D3A15.

25 William P. Barrett, "Dog Gets Top Financial Planner Honor," Forbes, May 14, 2009, accessed May 25, 2016, http://www.forbes.com/2009/05/14/americas-top-financial-planners-personal-finance-consumers-research-council.html.

26 Francis M. Kinniry Jr., Colleen M. Jaconetti, Michael A. DiJoseph, and Yan Zilbering, "Putting a Value on Your Value: Quantifying Vanguard Advisor's Alpha," Vanguard, March 2014, accessed May 26, 2016, http://vanguard.com/pdf/ISGQVAA.pdf.

27 J. Haden Werhan, "Wall Street's Yachts: Still Floating Finely," Thomas Wirig Doll Tax, Retirement & Wealth Advisors, June 18, 2015, accessed May 26, 2016, http://twdadvisors.com/wall-streets-yachts-still-floating-finely/.

Websites and Services Mentioned

Low-cost Brokers
Vanguard
Fidelity

Robo-advisors
Betterment
Wealthfront

Fee-only Certified Financial Planners
XYPlanningNetwork.com
Garrett Planning Network
NAPFA

Services
Blooom.com – Automatic 401(k) asset allocation
Brightscope.com – Retirement plan ratings (401(k), etc.)
FeeX.com – Compare mutual funds

Other
Dimensional Fund Advisors (DFA) dfaus.com

Acknowledgments

This book would have never happened or would have been one giant mess (or more of a mess than it is) without my wicked awesome team.

Thank you—Terry Turner, Barry Kaplan, Russ Baer, Stephanie Schwab, Kirk Du Plessis, Jeff Eagan, JennaLee Gallicchio, Charlie Cichetti, and Analyn Alforque.

About the Author

Scott Alan Turner is a popular podcaster and host of the *Financial Rock Star* show, where he helps people get out of debt faster, save more money, and retire rich. A self-proclaimed "money moron" in his early twenties, he got out of debt and became a self-made millionaire at age 35. Now, as an early retiree, he has the privilege of sharing his experiences about money with others and helping them achieve their goals in life—and becoming financial rock stars.

Scott lives in Dallas with his wife Katie and their twin toddlers, and Scott plays guitar in a rock-n-roll band.

To learn more about Scott, go to:

ScottAlanTurner.com/about

Made in the USA
Columbia, SC
01 December 2017